The Gen X Series

ENGLISH OLYMPIAD

3

Useful for English Olympiads Conducted at School, National & International Levels

Author
Sahil Gupta

Peer Reviewer
Manasvi Vohra

Strictly According to the Latest Syllabus of English Olympiad

V&S PUBLISHERS

Published by:

V&S PUBLISHERS

F-2/16, Ansari road, Daryaganj, New Delhi-110002
☎ 23240026, 23240027 • *Fax:* 011-23240028
Email: info@vspublishers.com • *Website:* www.vspublishers.com

Online Brandstore: amazon.in/vspublishers

Regional Office : Hyderabad
5-1-707/1, Brij Bhawan (Beside Central Bank of India Lane)
Bank Street, Koti, Hyderabad - 500 095
☎ 040-24737290
E-mail: vspublishershyd@gmail.com

Follow us on:

BUY OUR BOOKS FROM: AMAZON FLIPKART

© **Copyright:** *V&S PUBLISHERS*
ISBN 978-93-579407-1-9
New Edition

Printed at : Param Offsetters, Okhla, New Delhi–110020

Publisher's Note

The current decade has firmly established V&S Publishers as one of the Leading Publishers of General Trade Mass Appeal Books across popular genres along with Academic Books for school children. Having been in publishing trade for over 40 years we understand the need of the hour when it comes to Books. After successfully publishing over 600 titles in a rather short time span of 5 years and establishing a pan India network of booksellers & distributors including ecommerce platforms viz – Amazon, Flipkart etc; an extensive market research lead us to publishing our Bestselling Series ever – OLYMPIAD BOOKS.

The Olympiad Series launched 4 years back under our GEN X SERIES Imprint gained widespread popularity amongst students and teachers immediately owing to its rich, high quality content and unique presentation. Published for Classes 1-10 across subjects English, Maths, Science & Computers, these books are holistic in nature and unlike run of the mill workbooks in the market, which are mere replicas of one another, these books deal with the content in a much comprehensive manner. Recourse to the 'Principles of Applied Psychology of Student Learning' has been utilised to upgrade levels of conceptual understanding in all designated subjects among class 1 to 10 students.

Encouraged by this huge acceptability of our Olympiad Series among parents and students and after revolutionising the way Olympiad books were written and published, we at V&S Publishers decided to take this to the next level.

We present to you Brand New Edition of our book – **ENGLISH OLYMPIAD CLASS 3.**

Each book originally written by Subject Matter Expert, is now further Peer Reviewed by top School Teachers and HODs to eliminate the slightest of errors that were present earlier. Furthermore to ensure authenticity and accuracy of content the book is now completely revised and reformatted as per the guidelines of the examining body. The New and Revised Olympiad Book is now suited to Olympiad examinations conducted at School Level, National Level or International Level by any and all organisations/companies.

The New Edition of this English Olympiad Class 3 is written in a Guide like pattern with images and illustrations at every step & is divided into different sections. Each chapter comes with Basic Theory and Solved Examples. Multiple Choice Questions with their Answer Keys and Solutions are liberally included. In order to help students become aware of and to simulate the actual exam conditions, a bunch of OMR Sheets have been enclosed with the book as well.

Amalgamation of Technology with Content has always been at the forefront for V&S Publishers and our new Student Portal for Olympiad Practice–**www.vsexamprep.com** is further testimony to that. We recommend students logging in and using it to their benefit.

P.S. While every care has been taken to ensure correctness of content, if you come across any error, howsoever minor, anywhere in the book, do not hesitate to discuss with your teachers while pointing that out to us in no uncertain terms.

We wish you All The Best!

Contents

SECTION 1
WORD AND
STRUCTURE KNOWLEDGE

Spellings

1

It is essential to learn spellings to write correct English. Spellings in the English language follow no particular rule. No matter how strict a rule is, there will always be an exception. However, language experts have come up with the following important rules for spelling correctly:

Spelling Rules

'i' before 'e' except after c
This means that the letter 'i' should come before 'e' in a word. But the exception to this rule is that it does not apply if the letters 'e' and 'i' follow the alphabet c. For example, thief, brief, belief, relief, friend, etc.

Exception: their, science, receive, height.

Dropping final 'e'
We must drop the final 'e' before a suffix that begins with a vowel (a, e, i, o, u). But this is not the case if the suffix begins with a consonant.

Examples:

make + ing = making

surprise + ing = surprising

observe + ance = observance

entire + ly = entirely

close + ness = closeness

entertain + ment = entertainment

Changing final 'y' to 'i'
The final 'y' of a word changes to 'i' before a suffix. However, there is an exception to this rule if the suffix begins with an 'i'.

Examples:

merry + ment = merriment

mystery + ous = mysterious

baby + es = babies

Doubling the final consonant
When a word ends with a consonant and the suffix begins with a vowel, we usually double the final consonant.

Examples:

tap + ing = tapping

swim+ ing = swimming

begin + ing = beginning

Adding an 's' or 'es' to make words plural
When forming plurals, we usually add an 's' or 'es' to the word.

Examples:

pen - pens

tomato - tomatoes

But if a word ends with the 'f' sound, we make its plural by changing the 'f' to 'v' and adding an 'es'.

Examples:

knife - knives

wife - wives

leaf - leaves

Hard and soft 'c'
The letter 'c' can be pronounced softly as *ess* as in city, or as hard *kuh* as in candle. When the letter 'c' is pronounced as *ess*, it will come before 'i', 'e', and 'y'.

Examples:

centimetres, pencil, recent

Homophones
Homophones are words with the same sound but different spellings.

Examples:

I.   I will take a slice of cake, <u>too</u>.

     You need <u>to</u> take care of your health, mom.

     Two and <u>two</u> makes four.

II. <u>There</u> is a pond at the back of my house.

     The Smiths are going to move tomorrow. It is <u>their</u> house.

The silent 'e'

There are words that end in silent 'e', such as love, achieve and believe. When changing their spellings, look at the suffix. If the suffix begins with a vowel, drop the silent 'e' to form the final word. But if the suffix begins with a consonant, keep the 'e' in the final word that is formed.

Examples:

fame + ous = famous

like + ly = likely

care + ful = careful

Learning how to spell and write correctly comes with practice. It is important to keep a pocket dictionary handy so that one can refer to it. This can help one to become quite a spell master. The following is a list of the most commonly misspelt words:

Misspelling	Correct Spelling
acheive	achieve
arguement	argument
basicly	basically
begining	beginning
beleive, belive	believe
buisness	business
calender	calendar
commitee	committee
completly	completely
definately	definitely
dissapear	disappear
embarass	embarrass
enviroment	environment
finaly	finally
foriegn	foreign
fourty	forty
foward	forward
freind	friend
goverment	government
gaurd	guard
happend	happened
harrass, harrassment	harass, harassment
independant	independent
knowlege	knowledge
neccessary	necessary
noticable	noticeable
ocassion, occassion	occasion
peice	piece
realy	really
recieve	receive
religous	religious
rember, remeber	remember
sence	sense
succesful	successful
suprise	surprise
tommorow, tommorrow	tomorrow
tounge	tongue
truely	truly
unfortunatly	unfortunately
untill	until
wich	which

Practice Exercise

I. Choose the correct spelling option and fill in the blanks:

1. I will only have a _____ of the pie.
   - (a) peice
   - (b) piece
   - (c) peis
   - (d) peas

2. The _____ needs to be painted.
   - (a) ceiling
   - (b) selling
   - (c) cieling
   - (d) ceeling

3. We have a new _____.
   - (a) nieghbour
   - (b) nehbour
   - (c) nebour
   - (d) neighbour

4. It is _____ that Bharti did not attend my birthday party.
   - (a) surprisiing
   - (b) surpriseing
   - (c) surprysing
   - (d) surprising

5. Have you _____ the parcel?
   - (a) recieved
   - (b) receeved
   - (c) received
   - (d) reseeved

6. It is _____ Bhowmik's idea.
   - (a) completely
   - (b) completly
   - (c) complitely
   - (d) completelly

7. I was thrilled to see the _____ on Zara's face.
   - (a) excitement
   - (b) exytment
   - (c) excitement
   - (d) exciteement

8. Have you checked the _____ in the store room?
   - (a) supplys
   - (b) supplies
   - (c) suplies
   - (d) supplyies

9. 'When are you _____ promoted, son?', said the father.
   - (a) gating
   - (b) geting
   - (c) getting
   - (d) gatting

10. Rekha is buying a new _____ today.
    - (a) bicycle
    - (b) bycycle
    - (c) bycyycle
    - (d) bicyycle

11. India is an _____ country.
    - (a) indipendant
    - (b) independant
    - (c) independent
    - (d) indipendent

12. One must share one's _____ to increase it.
    - (a) knowledge
    - (b) knowlege
    - (c) nawlege
    - (d) nowledge

13. What a _____ scarf Piyu is wearing!
    - (a) lovlly
    - (b) lovly
    - (c) luvly
    - (d) lovely

14. The Sun is _____ now. We are late.
    - (a) setting
    - (b) seting
    - (c) sitting
    - (d) citing

15. You must _____ in your dreams.
    - (a) believ
    - (b) beeleev
    - (c) believe
    - (d) beleive

16. Dhruv was having an _____ with his mother when I called.
    - (a) arguement
    - (b) argument
    - (c) argewment
    - (d) rguement

17. Vimal is _____ a party on her birthday.
    - (a) planneing
    - (b) planeing
    - (c) planning
    - (d) planing

18. I will _____ come to your house tomorrow.
    - (a) definitly
    - (b) defenately
    - (c) definitely
    - (d) definitely

II. Choose the suitable homophones with the correct spellings and fill in the blanks:

1. She read the poem _____.
   - (a) alloud
   - (b) aloud
   - (c) allowed
   - (d) alowed

2. I am feeling _____ sleepy to complete this lesson.
   - (a) two
   - (b) to
   - (c) too
   - (d) twoo

3. What colour is her _____?
   - (a) hair
   - (b) hare
   - (c) here
   - (d) her

4. I wonder if the _____ will stop today.
   - (a) rein
   - (b) reign
   - (c) rain
   - (d) ren

5. The world needs people who want _____ .
   (a) peece (b) piece
   (c) piece (d) peace

6. Ali was _____ some money for parking in the wrong place.
   (a) fined (b) find
   (c) feind (d) fynd

III. Choose the correct plural spellings and fill in the blanks:

1. Shweta is going to change the _____ of the car.
   (a) tires (b) tyres
   (c) tyrees (d) tyress

2. Are there any good _____ nearby?
   (a) hotels (b) hotele
   (c) hoteles (d) hotel

3. They are constructing three _____ behind my home.
   (a) factoryes
   (b) factory
   (c) factories
   (d) factorys

4. How many _____ are there in the room?
   (a) boxess (b) boxes
   (c) boxis (d) box

5. The cows have given birth to three _____ .
   (a) calfs (b) calve
   (c) calf (d) calves

6. These are really nice _____ .
   (a) pitures (b) picture
   (c) picturees (d) pictures

◆◆◆

Collocations

2

There are certain expressions in the English language that come naturally to native English speakers. For them, there are words that go together. For example, native English speakers would rather say to break a law, do one's homework, rich culture, etc. These expressions are collocations. They are like word partners that generally go together and are used together frequently. The reason native speakers use a lot of collocations is that they make the language flow smoothly and naturally.

Collocations help us remember expressions. Keep the following in mind while learning collocations:

(i) Make an effort to identify collocations when you hear them.

(ii) When you hear a new word, try to form collocations with it.

(iii) Try to learn collocations as a single block of vocabulary instead of separate words.

Kinds of Collocations

Collocations are made by combining verbs, nouns, adjectives and adverbs. The following are the different kinds of collocations:

Adverb + Adjective

These are collocations that combine an adverb with an adjective.

Examples:

utterly confused

fully aware

Adjective + Noun

These are collocations that combine an adjective and a noun.

Examples:

regular exercise, heavy traffic

Noun + Noun

These are collocations that combine two nouns.

Examples:

a round of applause, a pack of cards

Verb + Noun

These are collocations that combine a verb and a noun.

Examples:

pay attention, save time

Verb + Adverb

These are collocations that combine a verb with an adverb.

Examples:

remember clearly, donate generously

Practice Exercise

I. Choose the most suitable collocation for the following sentences:

1. Mihisha could _____ time by driving to work.
   - (a) stand
   - (b) save
   - (c) have
   - (d) make

2. You should _____ your bills on time.
   - (a) have
   - (b) collect
   - (c) pay
   - (d) allow

3. Do you _____ calm in a difficult situation?
   - (a) make
   - (b) keep
   - (c) do
   - (d) break

4. Your efforts can really _____ a difference.
   - (a) have
   - (b) put
   - (c) do
   - (d) make

5. Sayani will _____ a presentation tomorrow.
   - (a) give
   - (b) have
   - (c) bring
   - (d) do

6. He whispered _____ in my ears that he wanted to leave.
   - (a) loudly
   - (b) pleasantly
   - (c) softly
   - (d) clearly

7. I was _____ with horror on reading this story.
   - (a) filled
   - (b) delighted
   - (c) driven
   - (d) happy

8. I _____ remember the day we met.
   - (a) softly
   - (b) distinctly
   - (c) pleasantly
   - (d) gently

9. Can you _____ a secret?
   - (a) make
   - (b) keep
   - (c) take
   - (d) show

10. He asked me if I had _____ a job?
    - (a) kept
    - (b) have
    - (c) got
    - (d) doing

11. He asked the shopkeeper for a _____ of soap.
    - (a) cube
    - (b) pack
    - (c) bottle
    - (d) bar

12. I felt a _____ of anger through my veins.
    - (a) rush
    - (b) surge
    - (c) flow
    - (d) blow

13. She is _____ a baby.
    - (a) wanting
    - (b) waiting for
    - (c) waiting
    - (d) expecting

14. We have a _____ weather today.
    - (a) nice
    - (b) strong
    - (c) kind
    - (d) gentle

15. I am _____ satisfied with the environment here.
    - (a) pleasantly
    - (b) happily
    - (c) deeply
    - (d) completely

16. They are offering a good _____ .
    - (a) pack
    - (b) deal
    - (c) offer
    - (d) option

17. I can afford a _____ holiday right now.
    - (a) cheap
    - (b) good
    - (c) luxury
    - (d) sound

18. You can _____ my car.
    - (a) drive
    - (b) ride
    - (c) have
    - (d) take

19. Are you going to _____ the exam?
    - (a) give
    - (b) make
    - (c) take
    - (d) plan

20. This system has _____ a lot of problems.
    - (a) added
    - (b) created
    - (c) brought
    - (d) caused

II. Identify the correct and incorrect usage of collocations in the following sentences:

(Note: 'T' stands for 'True' and 'F' stands for 'False'.)

1. Please do me a favour and hold this bag.
   You should not take advantage of your friends
   - (a) TT
   - (b) FF
   - (c) TF
   - (d) FT

2. The company has created a big loss.
   The company has made a big loss.
   - (a) TT
   - (b) FF
   - (c) TF
   - (d) FT

3. Do not eat fast food.

    Did you get a haircut?
    (a) TT   (b) FF
    (c) TF   (d) FT

4. You have to make a fine.

    You can catch the bus from Connaught Place.
    (a) TT   (b) FF
    (c) TF   (d) FT

5. Please make yourself comfortable.

    Please help yourself.
    (a) TT   (b) FF
    (c) TF   (d) FT

6. Shenu provided me with a compliment. Akriti saved me a seat in the hall.
    (a) TT   (b) FF
    (c) TF   (d) FT

7. The lights went dark at midnight.

    Who made first in your class?
    (a) TT   (b) FF
    (c) TF   (d) FT

8. I can make time for swimming every weekend.

    Preeti made a wrong conclusion.
    (a) TT   (b) FF
    (c) TF   (d) FT

9. I am extremely angry at Vineet's behaviour.

    Amanda is afraid to make a chance.
    (a) TT   (b) FF
    (c) TF   (d) FT

10. Will Sonia make the shopping alone?

    Ashraf made his homework himself.
    (a) TT   (b) FF
    (c) TF   (d) FT

Animals and Their Sounds, Food Habits and Homes

3

We see different types of animals around us, and they all have some common characteristics.

a. Eat food to survive:

   All animals need to eat to survive. They must consume and digest the food they get from plants and other animals.

b. Move from one place to the other:

   All animals can move around by themselves. They may move very slowly, and very little, but they can move. The act of moving from one place to another is called 'locomotion'.

c. Reproduce their offsprings:

   The act of bearing babies is called 'reproduction'. Different kinds of animals give birth to their offspring in different ways. Some give birth to living offspring (puppies, kittens, and cubs) and some (birds and snakes) lay eggs.

The Food Animals Eat

Different types of animals eat different kinds of food. So, we can group them according to the food they eat.

Animal	Food
Herbivores (cows, goats, camels, elephants, cockatoos, parakeets, and tortoises) **Granivores** (tree squirrels, crossbills, parrots, pigeons and doves) **Folivores** (sloths, okapis, koalas, and kakapos (a flightless type of parrot) are folivores	• Animals that eat only plants are called 'herbivores'. These animals eat leaves, shoots, flowers, fruits, seeds, and sometimes even wood. • The herbivores that mostly eat grains and seeds are called 'Granivores'. These animals have specialized teeth or beaks to make it easier to eat nuts and grains. • The herbivores that mainly eat leaves ('foliage') are called 'folivores'. The teeth and beaks of folivores help them in cutting up the leaves.
Carnivores (lions, tigers, wolves, sharks) **Predators** (lions and tigers) **Scavengers** (hyenas and vultures)	• The animals that eat other animals are called 'carnivores'. These animals have strong, sharp teeth called 'canines' which allow them to bite and tear the flesh of their food. • The carnivores that hunt other animals to eat them are called 'predators'. • The carnivores that do not hunt other animals, but eat the flesh of dead animals are called 'scavengers'.
Omnivores (dogs, cats, bears, chimpanzees, rats, and crows)	• The animals that eat both plants as well as other animals are called 'omnivores'. Chickens and other birds that eat worms as well as grain are called omnivores.

Homes for Animals

See the table below to know about animals and their homes

Animal	Home
Dog	Kennel
Fish	Aquarium
Hamster, Bird	Cage
Tortoise	Terrariums – Glass containers that are kept dry.
Rabbits, mongooses, snakes, moles, puffin	Burrows
Hares	Forms
Bees	Hives
Beavers	Lodge
Bears, bats	Caves
Lions, tigers, cheetahs, pandas, and foxes	Den
Monkeys, apes	Grove
Certain pets (tortoises, snails, frogs and butterflies)	Terrariums

Home for Farm Animals

Farm Animal	Home
Cow, Donkey, Mule	Barn
Horse	Stable
Pig	Sty
Sheep	Pen
Goat	Barn, Corral
Camel	Corral

Animal Sounds

Different animals make different sounds /noises to express their feelings of anger and affection. For example, we always hear cows say 'Moooo' and so we call that sound 'Moo'. We have always heard cats say 'Meow' and so we call this sound a 'Mew'. We say, for instance, the cow was mooing because it was hungry. Similarly, we use the word 'mew' for the sound a cat makes. Cats mew when they want to be petted.

Here is a list of animals and the sounds they make.

Animal	The Sound it Makes
Dog	Bark
Cat	Mew
Cow, Buffalo	Moo
Goat	Bleat
Bat	Screech
Bear	Growl
Bee	Buzz
Chicken	Cluck
Camel	Grunt
Hen	Cluck
Rooster	Crow
Monkeys, Chimpanzees	Chatter
Donkey	Bray
Dove, Pigeon	Coo
Ducks	Quack
Elephant	Trumpet
Frog	Croak
Geese	Cackle
Giraffe	Bleat
Sheep	Bleat
Horse	Neigh
Hogs	Grunt
Hyena	Laugh
Lion, Tiger	Roar

Mouse, Rat, Rabbit	Squeak
Peacock	Scream
Pig	Squeal
Owl	Hoot
Crow	Caw

Sparrow, Robin	Chirp
Snake	Hiss
Whale	Sing
Wolf	Howl
Swan	Cry

Practice Exercise

I. Fill in the blanks with the correct option given below.

1. Because they mainly eat bamboo shoots, the Greater Bamboo Lemur is a _____ animal.
   - (a) carnivorous
   - (b) omnivorous
   - (c) herbivorous
   - (d) granivorous

2. The cat-like animal, Fossa, is a ___ and mainly eats Lemurs and small animals.
   - (a) herbivore
   - (b) carnivore
   - (c) foliovore
   - (d) omnivore

3. The Cheetah used its sharp _____ to tear the Zebra's flesh.
   - (a) molars
   - (b) pre-molars
   - (c) incisors
   - (d) canines

4. The Pig _____ when it saw the wolf.
   - (a) squealed
   - (b) squeaked
   - (c) cried
   - (d) yelled

5. The Lion _____ at the trumpeting elephant.
   - (a) barked
   - (b) howled
   - (c) roared
   - (d) laughed

6. The night was cold and the Dog hid in its _____.
   - (a) aquarium
   - (b) stable
   - (c) sty
   - (d) kennel

7. The Giraffe is a folivore and mainly eats _____.
   - (a) branches
   - (b) grass
   - (c) leaves
   - (d) nuts

8. The Rabbit hid in its _____.
   - (a) burrow
   - (b) form
   - (c) nest
   - (d) corral

9. The Horse was missing from its _____.
   - (a) kennel
   - (b) burrow
   - (c) stable
   - (d) hive

10. The Mouse froze when it heard the snake _____.
   - (a) chatter
   - (b) growl
   - (c) croak
   - (d) hiss

II. Match the animal with their homes:

Animal	Home
1. Bee	(a) Cage
2. Goat	(b) Nest
3. Tortoise	(c) Corral
4. Lion	(d) Barn
5. Monkey	(e) Aquarium
6. Sheep	(f) Terrarium
7. Wasp	(g) Hive
8. Mule	(h) Den
9. Hamster	(i) Grove
10. Fish	(j) Pen

III. Understand the following statements and choose the correct option.

(Note: 'T' stands for 'True' and 'F' stands for 'False'.)

1. The villagers woke up to hear the wolf howl. The dogs were sleeping in their kennels.
   - (a) T T
   - (b) T F
   - (c) F T
   - (d) F F

2. The elephant ate the wasp. The wasp had been building its nest.
   - (a) T T
   - (b) T F
   - (c) F T
   - (d) F F

3. The cat was mewing loudly. The cat was hiding in its burrow.
   - (a) T T
   - (b) T F
   - (c) F T
   - (d) F F

4. The donkey is a beast of burden. It is a wild animal.
   - (a) T T
   - (b) T F
   - (c) F T
   - (d) F F

5. The okapi prefers to eat grains instead of leaves. They are wild animals.
   (a) T T   (b) T F
   (c) F T   (d) F F

6. We derive milk and leather from cows. They are tame animals.
   (a) T T   (b) T F
   (c) F T   (d) F F

7. The beaver built a burrow. The sparrows chirped when they heard the pig squeal.
   (a) T T   (b) T F
   (c) F T   (d) F F

8. The hyenas laughed as they circled the de The deer had been killed by a lion an ho ago.
   (a) T T   (b) T F
   (c) F T   (d) F F

9. The vulture killed the donkey and ate it. T horse neighed as it ran away.
   (a) T T   (b) T F
   (c) F T   (d) F F

10. The divers could hear the whales singing. the forest, the peacocks screamed.
    (a) T T   (b) T F
    (c) F T   (d) F F

◆◆◆

Parts of Body and Clothes

4

The Human Body

The human body is made up of three main parts: the head, the torso, and the limbs. As we grow, all three parts grow and get stronger. Some parts of the human body with a brief description of each have been given below.

Head

The head lies at the top of the body. Our head has a pair of eyes, a pair of ears, a nose, and a mouth.

Eye

Our eyes have a round eyeball covered with two eyelids. Our eyelids protect our eyes as they stop things from touching our eyeballs. Our eyelids also have tiny hair on them, called eyelashes. Eyelashes stop tiny objects from entering our eyes.

Hair

Hair is a non-living part of our body. It protects our head from the heat and the Sun's rays. Sometimes, our hair doesn't give us enough protection, and we need to wear clothes on our head. These are called headdresses or headgears. A headdress is used to protect our head and sometimes to decorate it as well. Caps and hats are headgears used by both men and women, while bonnets and scarves are usually used only by women.

Nose

We have a nose that sticks out in front of us. Our nose has two holes called nostrils, and we use them to smell things and to breathe in and out. Our nostrils also have tiny hair, called nose-hair, inside them to stop tiny objects from getting in. When we have a cold, our nose gets blocked with mucus and we need to clean it. We do this by blowing the mucus out, and we call this 'blowing our nose'.

Ear

On either side of the head, each of us has two ears. Our ears allow us to hear sounds, and their curved shape helps us to hear more than we would if they were flat. When we feel cold, we sometimes wear earmuffs or scarves on our ears to keep them warm. Earmuffs cover only our ears while scarves cover the sides of our heads.

Mouth

The mouth is the hole through which we eat, drink, and sometimes breathe. The mouth contains two rows of teeth, and a tongue and a pair of lips that cover them. We speak with the help of the tongue, mouth, and lips. We use our teeth to bite and chew food and the tongue helps us swallow. We call our two lips – the upper lip and the lower lip. Below the lower lip is our chin. Different people have chins of different sizes – some stick out and some are tiny.

Neck

The head is connected to the torso by the neck. All of us have necks, some necks are longer than others. The neck allows us to look around very easily because it can turn side to side. We wear items of clothing like ties and scarves as accessories for our necks.

The Torso

The torso is connected to the bottom part of the neck. It forms the middle part of our body. It also protects most of the insides of our body. On the outside, our torso is made up of three parts: the shoulders, the chest, and the stomach.

We have two shoulders, one on each side of the neck. They help us carry things, like bags, which we hang from them.

Chest

Below the shoulders is the chest. The chest protects our heart and lungs.

Below the chest is the abdomen. This is also called the belly through which we digest our food. On the inside, our stomach is like a bag. There are no bones guarding our stomach.

The Limbs

We have four limbs – two at the side of the torso and two below it. The first two are made up of an arm and a hand each. The last two are made up of a leg and a foot each. So, we have a left arm and a left hand, and a right arm and a right hand. We also have a left leg and left foot and a right leg and right foot.

Arms and Legs

Our arms are attached to our torso at each shoulder. Our legs are attached to our torso at its bottom. We use our arms to move things, to lift and carry things, and for many other tasks. We use our legs to run, walk, kick, jump, dance, and to do many other things. Each leg has two parts. The upper part is attached to the torso and called the thigh. When we sit down, both our thighs together form our lap. The lower part is called the lower leg. The knee joins the upper leg with the lower leg. The knee allows us to bend our leg. Below the lower leg is the foot. The place where the foot joins the leg is called the ankle. We can rotate our feet without moving our legs because our ankles let us do that. We have five toes on each foot. The largest toe, which looks a little like the thumb, is called the big toe. At the end of our toes we have toe nails. These are non-living parts of our bodies.

The bottom of our foot is called the sole. The skin here is harder than the skin in other parts of our body. The part of our sole exactly below our ankle is called the heel. So each foot has a sole and a heel.

Hand

At the end of each arm is a hand. The place where the hand joins the arm is called the wrist. We can rotate our hands without moving our arms because we have very flexible wrists. We use our hands to grip, hold, turn, pull, push, throw, hit, and do so many more things. Each hand has four fingers and one thumb. We have fingernails which are a non-living part of our body.

Fingers

We also have names for each finger in a hand. The first finger after the thumb is called the index finger or forefinger. It is also called the pointer finger as we use this finger to point at things. The finger after that is called the middle finger because it's exactly in the middle. The finger after that is called the ring finger because that is the finger we put rings on. And the last finger is the little finger because it's the smallest.

Palm:

The flat part on the inside of our hand is called the palm.

Clothes

We wear clothes for two reasons. First, we need to protect ourselves from the weather and our surroundings. Second, we use them to look good. The first reason is more important, and that is why the clothes people wear is different in different places.

In places that are very cold, the clothes that are worn are meant to keep the body warm. We have already spoken about ear-muffs and scarves. We also wear woolen caps or fur-caps to keep our heads warm. Remember, fur is made from the skin of other animals. We wear clothes made up of fur because they keep us very warm. But now, because too many animals are dying just so that we make our clothes, most people don't like wearing fur.

Clothes worn in cold regions

In cold places, we wear sweaters, suits, jackets and mufflers made out of wool. Sweaters, jackets and suits cover our torso, and mufflers cover our necks. They keep us warm because of the kind of cloth they are made from. We also have woolen pants that we wear to keep our legs warm. We can also cover our torsos with a shawl, a rectangular woolen cloth we wrap around our body.

Clothes worn in warmer regions

In warmer places, we wear clothes to keep cool as well as to protect our body from the heat of the Sun's rays. In such places, the clothes we wear are lighter, and looser. They are often made of cotton. In very hot places, we must take care to cover our heads or else our heads will get too hot. So we need some kind of head-gear.

In most places, we wear a cloth directly over our torso, so that it absorbs our sweat. This is because if we let our body stay wet for a very long time, we may fall sick. This cloth is called a vest, and is usually made of cotton.

Kinds of Clothes

We can have two types of clothes or garments.

The first is where we cover the torso with one garment and the legs with another. Examples of clothes of this kind are: Shirts, T-shirts, pants, half-pants, kurtas, pyjamas, and lungis. Shirts need to be worn and buttoned up around the torso. T-shirts and kurtas are pulled over the torso, and don't need to be buttoned up. Pants, half-pants, and pyjamas cover our legs and are pulled up the legs. Half-pants don't cover our lower legs.

The second kind of clothes we wear is when we cover the entire body with one garment. Examples of these are kimonos, sarees, frocks and dresses. Kimonos are worn by people in Japan. Sarees are worn by Indian women, and frocks and dresses are also women's clothing. Kimonos and Sarees wrap around the entire body while frocks and dresses are pulled over the body. In some warm countries, people wear sarongs. A sarong is a large cloth that can be wrapped around the torso and the legs, or only around the legs. So you can wear only a sarong around your entire body, or you can wear it with a shirt.

To protect our feet and keep them warm, we wear socks. Socks are usually woolen. Also, because we hurt ourselves when we walk on hard or uneven surfaces, we wear a protective covering called footwear on our feet. These coverings are made up of hard material (usually leather) and stop our feet from getting hurt. In cold places, they are often worn over socks. Different people prefer different footwear. Some kinds, like shoes, completely cover the feet. The other kinds, like slippers, leave the upper part of the feet open. In places where people have to walk on ice, for example, the bottom of their footwear has tiny sharp spikes that help them walk. So footwear is made a little differently depending on where you want to walk. When we don't wear footwear, we walk around in bare feet.

Practice Exercise

I   Fill in the blanks with the correct option:

1. The boy _____ his _____ to start whistling.
   - (a) twisted, ankle
   - (b) pursed, lips
   - (c) bent, elbow
   - (d) wiggled, toes

2. The waiter bent his _____ and carried the heavy tray on his _____.
   - (a) neck, head
   - (b) elbows, forearms
   - (c) knees, lower legs
   - (d) lips, tongue

3. The football player kicked the ball with his _____.
   - (a) teeth
   - (b) head
   - (c) ankle
   - (d) elbow

4. The ball hit John on the _____, just above his stomach.
   - (a) torso
   - (b) legs
   - (c) ankles
   - (d) elbows

5. Jacob was getting late, and so he put on an old _____ and a pair of pants.
   - (a) pyjamas
   - (b) saree
   - (c) shirt
   - (d) sarong

6. The day was cold, and so Tim wore a pair of _____ over his ears.
   - (a) trousers
   - (b) shirts
   - (c) caps
   - (d) ear-muffs

7. Lindsay had caught cold, and so she was always _____ her _____.
   - (a) wiping, feet
   - (b) turning, neck
   - (c) holding, hands
   - (d) blowing, nose

8. Ravi was feeling hot and so he decided to wear a _____.
   - (a) jacket
   - (b) shawl
   - (c) t-shirt
   - (d) muffler

9. Susan sat down with a baby on her _____.
   - (a) neck
   - (b) lap
   - (c) knuckles
   - (d) feet

10. Marlene _____ on the bed in her _____.
    - (a) ate, digits
    - (b) slept, kimono
    - (c) jumped, knees
    - (d) knocked, knuckles

II.   Match the following parts of body with its function.

Parts of Body	Function
1. Index Finger	(a) Walking
2. Knuckle	(b) Smelling
3. Lips	(c) Seeing
4. Ears	(d) Protects the heart
5. Eyes	(e) Digesting food
6. Nose	(f) Pointing
7. Chest	(g) Lifting
8. Stomach	(h) Whistling
9. Arms	(i) Knocking
10. Legs	(j) Hearing

III.   Choose which of the statements is/are correct.

(Note: 'T' stands for 'True' and 'F' stands for 'False'.)

1. It was a cold day and James decided to wear a sarong to work. Jack was feeling cold too, and he wore a sweater.
   - (a) T T
   - (b) T F
   - (c) F T
   - (d) F F

2. In winter, men wear coats. In summer, they wear Sarees and Frocks.
   - (a) T T
   - (b) T F
   - (c) F T
   - (d) F F

3. Timmy bent his elbows to kick the ball. The ball hit John in his stomach, just below his knees.
   - (a) T T
   - (b) T F
   - (c) F T
   - (d) F F

4. Shanti held the spoon firmly between her index finger and her thumb. She bent her elbow as she lifted the spoon to her mouth.
   - (a) T T
   - (b) T F
   - (c) F T
   - (d) F F

Sunil pursed his lips and whistled a tune. But because his ears were blocked, it sounded strange.

(a) T T   (b) T F
(c) F T   (d) F F

Anil wore a scarf because his feet were cold. He also wrapped a shoe around his neck.

(a) T T   (b) T F
(c) F T   (d) F F

Because he had walked so much, the soles of his feet hurt. His thighs also hurt because of the exercise.

(a) T T   (b) T F
(c) F T   (d) F F

8. He took off his socks without taking off his shoes. He took off his shoes without taking off his socks.

(a) T T   (b) T F
(c) F T   (d) F F

9. Mike made a fist to knock at the door. His wedding ring on his middle finger hurt him.

(a) T T   (b) T F
(c) F T   (d) F F

10. Peter closed his eyebrows and lay down to sleep. He had just worn a muffler to keep warm.

(a) T T   (b) T F
(c) F T   (d) F F

Basic Emotions

5

What are emotions?

Animals have the sense to understand the emotions of others. This is because when we feel, we can express it through different ways of expressions. When we are happy, we smile; when we are frightened, we perspire a lot; and when we are angry, our faces sometimes turn red and we get hot-headed. We have learnt to see these feelings as signs of our emotions. When we see these signs in others, we can understand their emotions. Others can also recognize our emotions in the same way. Our emotions are very strongly related to our expressions, and we can see them most of the time.

For example, when we are not speaking strictly, we sometimes use the words 'feelings' and 'emotions' to mean the same thing. So when we say 'Ram should share his feelings', what we mean is that Ram should show people his emotions. Also, when we say 'Shyam hurt my feelings', we mean that Shyam caused me to feel hurt. In other words, Shyam made me feel the emotion of sadness.

Basic Emotions

Basic emotions are those emotions that all human beings feel and express in almost the same way. If you see these emotions expressed, you will almost always be able to recognize them. They are also so different from each other that you cannot get confused between them. So, for example, imagine that you stepped into a puddle of mud by mistake. Which emotion would you feel: anger, joy, sadness, or disgust? The correct answer is disgust, and it's clear that the other options are wrong.

See the sentence below:

Jack was *glad* to see the flower.

If we change it to 'Jack was *happy* to see the flower', the meaning of the sentence doesn't change much. But to say 'Jack was *overjoyed* to see the flower' means that seeing the flower made Jack extremely and uncontrollably happy. So, we cannot replace 'glad' with 'overjoyed'. Therefore,

'happiness' is the basic emotion here, because it can be used in place of the other two emotions without being incorrect.

Types of Basic Emotions?

There are six basic emotions: happiness, sadness, anger, disgust, fear, and surprise.

Happiness

Happiness is the emotion we feel when something good happens. When we are happy, we tend to smile, laugh, maybe even whistle or sing or dance. Some weak forms of 'happiness' are 'gladness', 'cheerfulness', and 'merriness'. These are used in the following examples:

The boy was singing *cheerfully*.

The lady was *glad* to see the boy so happy.

Some strong forms of 'happiness' are 'being delighted', 'being overjoyed', and 'being elated'. These are used in the following examples:

The boy was *delighted* to find that he got his favourite toy as a gift.

The girl was *overjoyed* to find that she came first in class.

The cricket team was *elated* at having won the World Cup.

Sadness

Sadness is the emotion we feel when something bad happens. When we are sad, we tend to cry, our lips begin to tremble, we don't feel like doing anything (nothing feels nice), and our body droops down. Some weak forms of 'sadness' are 'feeling downhearted', 'feeling gloomy', and 'feeling listless'. These are used in the following examples:

The new videogame he had ordered was not delivered. This made Rama feel *listless*.

[To be listless means to not feel like doing anything]

It was raining, and Ravi couldn't play cricket. This made him feel quite *gloomy*.

On seeing the poor beggar maid, Manasvi felt *downhearted*.

Some strong forms of 'sadness' are 'grief, 'misery', and 'woe'. These are used in the following examples:

Avinash felt *miserable* when he failed in his yearly exam..

Luke's dog Droopy died three years ago. This still causes Luke much *grief*.

Suraj was *woeful* because he had just lost a lot of money.

Anger

We mostly feel anger when we see that something has happened against our wishes or against what we feel as being right or just. When we are angry, our lips get tight, we frown, and we sometimes clench our fists. We may also scream, yell, or throw a tantrum.

Some weak forms of 'anger' are 'annoyance', 'irritation', and 'displeasure'. These are used in the following examples:

Kiran was *annoyed* because her pencil nib kept breaking throughout the day.

Sarah's little brother loved to play with her toys. This *irritated* Sarah.

The sight of all that pollution caused Reema much *displeasure*.

Some strong forms of 'anger' are 'rage', and 'fury'. These are used in the following examples:

The red fence made the bull very angry. The *raging* bull charged at the fence.

The Principal was *furious* with the boy who cheated.

Disgust

We feel disgust when we come across something that is unpleasant and offends us. For instance, we feel disgust when we smell or taste something horrible (like rotten food), touch something dirty (like somebody else's snot), or see something that we feel unpleasant (like dog poop). We feel disgust when someone behaves in an unpleasant way too or when someone cheats other people, or hurts them.

Some weak forms of 'disgust' are 'dislike' and 'distaste'. These are used in the following examples:

At lunch, John let his food drip all over his beard. Mario looked at John with *distaste*.

Jacob thinks boxing is a violent and *distasteful* game.

Anne *disliked* the way her classmates kept eating her tiffin without asking her.

A strong form of 'disgust' is 'hatred'. Consider the following examples:

Jack *hated* the way his classmates bullied the weaker students.

Mia always tattles to the teacher and so the other girls *hate* her.

Fear

Fear is the emotion we feel when we are in some danger. When we are afraid, we may sweat a lot, breathe faster, and our heart beats faster too. When we feel fear, we become 'frightened'. This is why anything that makes us feel fear is called 'frightening'.

Some weak forms of 'fear' are 'worry' and 'doubt'. These are used in the following examples:

Margaret was *worried* that the audience would not like her song.

Everyone noticed she was *worrying* because she kept biting her fingernails.

Peter felt *doubtful* about passing his end-term exams.

Some strong forms of 'fear' are 'terror' and 'panic'. These are used in the following examples:

Abel is *terrified* of spiders – he faints when he sees them.

Thunder and lightning *terrify* little children.

Nigel began to *panic* when he saw the car speed towards him.

The passengers *panicked* when the bus lost control.

Surprise

Surprise is what we feel when something that we didn't expect happens. We are also surprised when we wait for something to happen, but it does not.

And when we are surprised, our eyes widen and we raise our eyebrows without realizing it.

A weak form of 'surprise' is 'curiosity'. Consider the following examples:

- The gas balloon kept rising instead of falling, and the child found this very curious.
- Ravi found it *curious* that the magician could keep pulling so many rabbits out of such a small hat.

A strong form of 'surprise' is 'amazement' and 'shock'. Consider the following examples.

- It was *shocking* to know that the money was stolen by a policeman.
- It came as a *shock* to Rahul when he learnt that his costly new car was stolen.
- Shriya was *amazed* at how easily she finished answering all the examination questions.
- Every time Sachin Tendulkar bats, he *amazes* us with his skill.
- In every movie, Vera manages to *amaze* the audience with her beauty.

Remember, we often use the word 'shock' for something surprising and bad, and we often use the word 'amaze' for something surprising and good.

Practice Exercise

I   Fill in the blank with the correct emotion:

1. Ramesh finally got the job he had been trying to get. This made him extremely _____.
   - (a) Sad
   - (b) Afraid
   - (c) Happy
   - (d) Disgusted

2. Susan was _____ of the big and angry-looking dog.
   - (a) Surprised
   - (b) Afraid
   - (c) Disgusted
   - (d) Sad

3. Reena's son had spilled jam all over the floor. She came home, stepped on the jam, and felt very _____.
   - (a) Listless
   - (b) Happy
   - (c) Disgusted
   - (d) Sad

4. John is a lion trainer. You and I would find this job very _____.
   - (a) Frightening
   - (b) Cheerful
   - (c) Annoying
   - (d) Distasteful

5. On seeing Megan's sweet smile, Alfred immediately _____.
   - (a) Got furious
   - (b) Got terrified
   - (c) Became miserable
   - (d) Cheered up

6. The hunter was _____ that his prey had got away.
   - (a) Overjoyed
   - (b) Terrified
   - (c) Glad
   - (d) Furious

7. The children sat around _____ during recess because the teacher didn't let them play outside.
   - (a) Shockingly
   - (b) Listlessly
   - (c) Curiously
   - (d) Feeling delighted

8. The beggar was _____ to find a little money lying on the road.
   - (a) Afraid
   - (b) Sad
   - (c) Surprised
   - (d) Disgusted

9. The poor man was _____ to find such a large amount of money on the road.
   - (a) Shocked
   - (b) Amazed
   - (c) Full of hatred
   - (d) Miserable

10. The players were _____ because their team had won.
    - (a) Overjoyed
    - (b) Cheerful
    - (c) Disgusted
    - (d) Shocked

II.   See the underlined word/emotion given in the questions and choose the correct option to match it with the basic emotion:

1. Agnes was <u>disheartened</u> by how easily people get annoyed.
   - (a) Happiness
   - (b) Sadness
   - (c) Fear
   - (d) Surprise

2. Jillian is <u>overjoyed</u> because she managed to overcome her fears.
   - (a) Fear
   - (b) Happiness
   - (c) Anger
   - (d) Surprise

3. Tom ate his vegetables irritated, but he ate his cake <u>cheerfully</u>.
   - (a) Disgust
   - (b) Anger
   - (c) Sadness
   - (d) Happiness

4. Mary was <u>worried</u> about how easily she got shocked.
   - (a) Happiness
   - (b) Surprise
   - (c) Fear
   - (d) Sadness

5. The lad found the way the pigeons panicked very <u>curious</u>.
   - (a) Surprise
   - (b) Anger
   - (c) Disgust
   - (d) Happiness

6. Jack was irritated at how <u>listless</u> his classmates were.
   - (a) Happiness
   - (b) Surprise
   - (c) Fear
   - (d) Sadness

7. The <u>panic</u> Susan felt when she saw clowns annoyed her parents.
   - (a) Anger
   - (b) Surprise
   - (c) Disgust
   - (d) Fear

8. Jill's <u>hatred</u> of injustice left her parents elated.
   - (a) Disgust
   - (b) Surprise
   - (c) Fear
   - (d) Sadness

9. Ronaldo's <u>misery</u> because he failed his test was overcome by his delight at winning the match.
   - (a) Happiness
   - (b) Sadness
   - (c) Fear
   - (d) Disgust

10. Ali found John's elation at Margaret's woe <u>distasteful</u>.
    (a) Fear
    (b) Sadness
    (c) Disgust
    (d) Happiness

III. Determine whether the underlined emotions are strong forms or weak forms of their basic emotions:

1. Jack was <u>overjoyed</u> at the thought of shifting to America. He was a little <u>worried</u> about making new friends.
    (a) Stronger, Stronger
    (b) Stronger, Weaker
    (c) Weaker, Stronger
    (d) Weaker, Weaker

2. Alex looked rather <u>gloomy</u>. He had lost his books, and that made his parents <u>furious</u>.
    (a) Stronger, Stronger
    (b) Stronger, Weaker
    (c) Weaker, Stronger
    (d) Weaker, Weaker

3. David <u>disliked</u> carrots. He found it <u>curious</u> that his mom always gave him carrots for dinner.
    (a) Stronger, Stronger
    (b) Stronger, Weaker
    (c) Weaker, Stronger
    (d) Weaker, Weaker

4. Rambo was <u>doubtful</u> about how real Rita's <u>shock</u> was.
    (a) Stronger, Stronger
    (b) Stronger, Weaker
    (c) Weaker, Stronger
    (d) Weaker, Weaker

5. The sight of Janet's <u>grief</u> made Julie feel <u>miserable</u>.
    (a) Stronger, Stronger
    (b) Stronger, Weaker
    (c) Weaker, Stronger
    (d) Weaker, Weaker

6. Sharon began to <u>panic</u> when she saw Desmond fly into a <u>rage</u>.
    (a) Stronger, Stronger
    (b) Stronger, Weaker
    (c) Weaker, Stronger
    (d) Weaker, Weaker

7. Michael <u>hated</u> sea-food, and got <u>furious</u> when his parents ordered prawn for dinner.
    (a) Stronger, Stronger
    (b) Stronger, Weaker
    (c) Weaker, Stronger
    (d) Weaker, Weaker

8. The prisoner <u>whistled</u> merrily, much to the jailor's <u>irritation</u>.
    (a) Stronger, Stronger
    (b) Stronger, Weaker
    (c) Weaker, Stronger
    (d) Weaker, Weaker

9. Scientists are <u>amazed</u> at how quick animals become when they are <u>terrified</u>.
    (a) Stronger, Stronger
    (b) Stronger, Weaker
    (c) Weaker, Stronger
    (d) Weaker, Weaker

10. His <u>shocking</u> behaviour caused his friends much <u>displeasure</u>.
    (a) Stronger, Stronger
    (b) Stronger, Weaker
    (c) Weaker, Stronger
    (d) Weaker, Weaker

The names of persons, places, animals or things are known as nouns. In other words, naming words are called nouns.

Naming words such as cup, hat, mug, umbrella, part, pen, scarf, bag and door are all nouns.

See more examples in the table below.

Person	Place	Animal	Thing
father	home	owl	book
actor	office	dog	envelope
teacher	school	zebra	telephone
artist	airport	fish	ticket

Types of nouns

Nouns are of the following kinds:

Common Nouns

Common Nouns refer to the general or commonly used names of a person, place, animal, thing or even a quality. A common noun is spelt with small letters.

Examples are: teacher, tent, bird, hill, chair, etc.

Words like girl, city, and animal are nouns. But we cannot say that the noun 'city' refers to any specific city. 'City' is a name that we give to all cities of one kind, that is, cities in general.

Such nouns are thus referred to as common nouns.

Abstract Nouns

Abstract Nouns refer to the names of things that one cannot touch. One can only feel the quality or state of such nouns. Examples of abstract nouns include beauty, honesty, happiness, pleasure, freedom, childhood, etc.

Proper Nouns

These nouns are the specific names of people and places. They are always spelt with a capital initial letter.

Consider the following sentences:

Mrs. Prasad was late for her class.

Goa is the smallest state in India.

The girl and her mother are moving to Lincoln Street.

In the first sentence, Mrs Prasad is a proper noun as it refers to a particular person. It is the name of a specific person. Similarly, Goa and India refer to a particular state and country respectively. Again, in the third sentence, we refer to a particular street.

Days of the week, months of the year and names of festivals are also proper nouns. They are also spelt with a capital initial letter.

Examples of proper nouns include Winston Churchill, Sikkim, the Great Wall of China, Park Road, Pacific Ocean, Sunday, January, Christmas, etc.

Collective Nouns

When we want to refer to a group of persons, things or animals collectively, we use collective nouns. Examples of collective nouns include army, herd, bunch, crowd, etc. Words such as family, choir, team and society are collective nouns.

Practice Exercise

I. Pick the odd noun out:

1. Sargam, Eiffel Tower, December, mobile
   - (a) Sargam
   - (b) Eiffel Tower
   - (c) December
   - (d) mobile

2. table, wisdom, book, glass
   - (a) table
   - (b) wisdom
   - (c) book
   - (d) glass

3. violin, family, bunch, crowd
   - (a) violin
   - (b) family
   - (c) bunch
   - (d) crowd

4. beach, plane, hills, the Himalayas
   - (a) beach
   - (b) plane
   - (c) hills
   - (d) the Himalayas

5. honesty, beauty, eggs, childhood
   - (a) honesty
   - (b) beauty
   - (c) eggs
   - (d) childhood

6. tree, knife, aeroplane, Mr. Das
   - (a) tree
   - (b) knife
   - (c) aeroplane
   - (d) Mr. Das

II. Identify the common nouns in the given sentences:

1. The teacher is reading a book.
   - (a) teacher, book
   - (b) is reading
   - (c) The
   - (d) a

2. She ate the sandwich quickly.
   - (a) She
   - (b) ate
   - (c) sandwich
   - (d) quickly

3. The bicycle belongs to me.
   - (a) The
   - (b) bicycle
   - (c) belongs
   - (d) me

4. The sky is filled with stars.
   - (a) sky, stars
   - (b) The, with
   - (c) is, stars
   - (d) filled, sky

5. The fly is sitting on the cake.
   - (a) fly, cake
   - (b) sitting, fly
   - (c) on, cake
   - (d) the, on

6. We climbed on the hill.
   - (a) We
   - (b) hill
   - (c) on
   - (d) climbed

7. The butterfly is a beautiful insect.
   - (a) beautiful, insect
   - (b) butterfly, insect
   - (c) butterfly, beautiful
   - (d) the butterfly

8. The chef is making soup.
   - (a) The
   - (b) chef, soup
   - (c) is making
   - (d) chef, the

9. The tomatoes are in the basket.
   - (a) tomatoes, are
   - (b) basket, in
   - (c) tomatoes, basket
   - (d) in

10. She is writing a book on the Taj Mahal.
    - (a) Taj Mahal
    - (b) book
    - (c) is writing
    - (d) she

11. There is no water in the jug.
    - (a) There, water
    - (b) water, jug
    - (c) There, in
    - (d) water, there

12. The rabbit came out of his hat.
    - (a) rabbit, hat
    - (b) came, rabbit
    - (c) came, hat
    - (d) came

III. Choose the type of underlined nouns in the given sentences:

1. The <u>princess</u> is marrying the prince tomorrow.
   - (a) Proper noun
   - (b) Common noun
   - (c) Abstract noun
   - (d) Collective noun

2. <u>Ted</u> is very happy at his new office.
   - (a) Proper noun
   - (b) Common noun
   - (c) Abstract noun
   - (d) Collective noun

3. <u>Happiness</u> comes by helping people.
   - (a) Proper noun
   - (b) Common noun
   - (c) Abstract noun
   - (d) Collective noun

4. The <u>crew</u> of sailors left the inn.
   - (a) Proper noun
   - (b) Common noun
   - (c) Abstract noun
   - (d) Collective noun

5. Do you have some <u>food</u>?
   - (a) Proper noun
   - (b) Common noun
   - (c) Abstract noun
   - (d) Collective noun

6. There is a red building next to my <u>house</u>.
   - (a) Proper noun
   - (b) Common noun
   - (c) Abstract noun
   - (d) Collective noun

7. India got <u>freedom</u> in the year 1947.
   - (a) Proper noun
   - (b) Common noun
   - (c) Abstract noun
   - (d) Collective noun

8. I am going to <u>Dalhousie</u> during summer vacation.
   (a) Proper noun   (b) Common noun
   (c) Abstract noun   (d) Collective noun

9. Dhruv loves reading books written by JK <u>Rowling</u>.
   (a) Proper noun   (b) Common noun
   (c) Abstract noun   (d) Collective noun

10. <u>Peggy</u> is afraid of the dog.
   (a) Proper noun   (b) Common noun
   (c) Abstract noun   (d) Collective noun

11. The <u>Pacific Ocean</u> is the largest ocean in the world.
   (a) Proper noun
   (b) Common noun
   (c) Abstract noun
   (d) Collective noun

12. Purnima plays <u>violin</u> very well.
   (a) Proper noun
   (b) Common noun
   (c) Abstract noun
   (d) Collective noun

Pronouns

7

Pronoun is a word which takes the place of a noun in a sentence.

We need not use the same noun again and again in a set of sentences. We can use pronouns to make things simple.

For example,

Asra is a pilot. Asra wears a uniform. Asra is very intelligent.

In the above sentence, we need not use Asra's name in the second and third sentences. We can use a pronoun here, instead. We can replace the noun Asra with the pronoun she. Thus, the sentence can be rewritten as follows:

Asra is a pilot. She wears a uniform. She is very intelligent

Before you use pronouns, you must make sure that the pronoun must match in number and gender with the noun that it stands for.

Types of Pronouns

The following are different types of pronouns.

Personal Pronoun

Personal pronouns refer to the person who is speaking *(I, me, we, us),* the person who is spoken to *(you)*, and the person or thing who is spoken about *(he, she, it, they, him, her, them).*

Examples

I am eight years old.

She is going to the station.

You are a very helpful person.

Reflexive Pronoun

Adding *self* or *selves* to personal pronouns will form reflexive pronouns.

Examples:

My mother will do the plumbing work herself.

We should do our work ourselves.

Interrogative Pronoun

We use interrogative pronouns to ask questions. Who, whom, what, when, where and how are interrogative pronouns. They refer to the things whose answers we do not know and want to find out.

Examples:

Who is coming to the house tonight?

What is your name?

Demonstrative Pronoun

We use demonstrative pronouns to point at an object or place. This, these, that and those are demonstrative pronouns. This and these are used for nouns that are near; that and those are used for nouns that are far. This and that are used for singular nouns; that and those are used for plural nouns.

Examples:

This is a house.

Those are cups.

Possessive Pronoun

We use possessive pronouns to show that something belongs to someone. For example, mine, ours, his, yours, theirs and hers are used to show possession.

This house is mine.

The books are hers.

Practice Exercise

I. Choose the correct pronoun from the options and fill in the blanks:

1. _____ helped the old man cross the road.
   - (a) This
   - (b) When
   - (c) She
   - (d) Me

2. Will you lend _____ some money?
   - (a) me
   - (b) you
   - (c) I
   - (d) whom

3. They are enjoying _____ .
   - (a) yourself
   - (b) themselves
   - (c) oneself
   - (d) myself

4. _____ is the *saree* that I wore on the wedding.
   - (a) This
   - (b) These
   - (c) When
   - (d) Who

5. God helps those who help _____ .
   - (a) myself
   - (b) themselves
   - (c) oneself
   - (d) yourselves

6. I will call _____ tomorrow.
   - (a) they
   - (b) he
   - (c) them
   - (d) us

7. _____ is your class teacher?
   - (a) These
   - (b) Who
   - (c) That
   - (d) Those

8. _____ am ten years old.
   - (a) She
   - (b) You
   - (c) They
   - (d) I

9. _____ pencil is this?
   - (a) Whose
   - (b) Whom
   - (c) Who
   - (d) These

10. _____ will get late for the party.
    - (a) Us
    - (b) We
    - (c) Them
    - (d) Who

11. They have invited _____ to dinner.
    - (a) I
    - (b) we
    - (c) us
    - (d) these

12. _____ is the house that I want to buy.
    - (a) This
    - (b) These
    - (c) Where
    - (d) Whose

13. She looked at _____ in the mirror.
    - (a) myself
    - (b) herself
    - (c) yourself
    - (d) oneself

14. The keys belong to her. They are _____ .
    - (a) mine
    - (b) hers
    - (c) yours
    - (d) theirs

15. Where are _____ going?
    - (a) this
    - (b) she
    - (c) us
    - (d) you

II. Pick the odd pronoun out:

1. I, She, Me, You
   - (a) I
   - b. She
   - (c) Me
   - (d) You

2. myself, him, himself, yourself
   - (a) myself
   - (b) him
   - (c) himself
   - (d) yourself

3. Mine, this, that, those
   - (a) Mine
   - (b) This
   - (c) That
   - (d) Those

4. yours, theirs, his, her
   - (a) Yours
   - (b) Theirs
   - (c) His
   - (d) Her

5. Who, They, Whom, Whose
   - (a) Who
   - (b) They
   - (c) Whom
   - (d) Whose

III. Choose the kind of pronoun the underlined word is:

1. These buildings are red in colour.
   - (a) Reflexive pronoun
   - (b) Personal pronoun
   - (c) Interrogative pronoun
   - (d) Demonstrative pronoun

2. She lives alone in the apartment.
   - (a) Personal pronoun
   - (b) Interrogative pronoun
   - (c) Demonstrative pronoun
   - (d) Reflexive pronoun

3. I was talking to myself.
   - (a) Demonstrative pronoun
   - (b) Possessive pronoun
   - (c) Reflexive pronoun
   - (d) Interrogative pronoun

4. The farm is <u>ours</u>.
   (a) Demonstrative pronoun
   (b) Possessive pronoun
   (c) Reflexive pronoun
   (d) Interrogative pronoun

5. Did <u>you</u> speak to them?
   (a) Personal pronoun
   (b) Possessive pronoun
   (c) Reflexive pronoun
   (d) Interrogative pronoun

IV. Justify the usage of pronouns in the given sentences:

(Note: 'T' stands for 'True' and 'F' stands for 'False'.)

1. He was feeling tired.
   You are an honest man.
   (a) TT   (b) FF
   (c) TF   (d) FT

2. The tools belong to you. They are your.
   The kite belongs to her. It is hers.
   (a) TT   (b) FF
   (c) TF   (d) FT

3. His son is taller than me.
   You are shorter than I am.
   (a) TT   (b) FF
   (c) TF   (d) FT

4. He called out your name.
   Who is calling my name?
   (a) TT   (b) FF
   (c) TF   (d) FT

5. This is you bag.
   James is absent today. But he will come tomorrow.
   (a) TT   (b) FF
   (c) TF   (d) FT

Verbs

8

The part of speech used to describe an action, state, or occurrence is called verb.

Example:

He is *writing* a letter.

In the above example, the verb '*write*' tells us about the action (writing) of the subject (he). A verb has its subject in a sentence and tells us what its subject does, did or will do.

Most verbs describe action, such verbs are called 'dynamic verbs', for example *write, eat, run, speak*. Some verbs describe state of something, such verbs are called 'stative verb' and are not usually used in continuous tense; for example, *be, impress, please, surprise, belong to, consist of, resemble, seem.*

Example:

He *works* in a factory. (action)

I *bought* a computer. (action)

John *seems* happy. (state)

He *resembles* his brother. (state)

Some verbs can be used as dynamic verbs as well as stative verbs.

Example:

She *looks* very beautiful. (stative verb)

She *looked* at the black board. (dynamic verb)

Main Verbs and Helping Verbs (Auxiliary)

A sentence can have both a main verb and a helping verb (auxiliary verb).

Main verb: A verb which shows the action of the subject. Main verbs can stand alone, or they can be helped along by some other verbs (auxiliary verbs, i.e. write, buy, eat, etc.)

Helping verb: A verb which supports the main verb to form the structure of a sentence, according to a specific tense, is called a helping verb or auxiliary verb, e.g., is, am, have, was, had, is, will, etc.

A main verb has real meaning and tells more about the action while a helping verb has no (or little) meaning. See the examples below.

She *is eating* an apple. ('eat' is the main verb while 'is' is the helping verb)

She *was eating* an apple. ('eat' is the main verb while 'was' is the helping verb)

Irregular Verbs

Irregular verbs are those which do not follow the rule of forming past tenses just by adding the suffix '-d' or '-ed.' You have to remember the exact past tense of these verbs since there is no common formula.

For example, the past tense of eat is not 'eated' but ate.

Some of them follow a pattern. See examples below:

drink-drank, spring-sprang etc.

But these rules don't apply to all the irregular verbs, the only way to know all of these is to memorize them.

Some common irregular verbs are:

Present	Past
Be	Was, Were
Beat	Beat
Become	Became
Begin	Began
Bend	Bent
Bleed	Bled
Blow	Blew
Break	Broke
Bring	Brought
Build	Built
Burn	Burnt
Buy	Bought

Catch	Caught	Lose	Lost
Choose	Chose	Make	Made
Come	Came	Meet	Met
Cost	Cost	Pay	Paid
Cut	Cut	Prove	Proved
Dig	Dug	Put	Put
Dive	Dived	Read	Read
Do	Did	Rise	Rose
Drink	Drank	Run	Ran
Drive	Drove	Saw	Sawed
Eat	Ate	Say	Said
Fall	Fell	See	Saw
Feel	Felt	Sell	Sold
Fight	Fought	Send	Sent
Find	Found	Show	Showed
Fly	Flew	Sing	Sang
Get	Got	Sink	Sank
Give	Gave	Sit	Sat
Go	Went	Sleep	Slept
Grind	Ground	Speak	Spoke
Grow	Grew	Speed	Sped
Hang	Hung	Spend	Spent
Have	Had	Spread	Spread
Hear	Heard	Spring	Sprang
Hide	Hid	Stand	Stood
Hit	Hit	Steal	Stole
Hold	Held	Swim	Swam
Hurt	Hurt	Take	Took
Keep	Kept	Teach	Taught
Kneel	Knelt or kneeled	Tell	Told
Knit	Knit	Think	Thought
Know	Knew	Throw	Threw
Lay	Laid	Understand	Understood
Lead	Led	Upset	Upset
Leap	Leapt or leaped	Wear	Wore
Leave	Left	Weep	Wept
Lend	Lent	Win	Won
Let	Let	Wind	Wound
Lie (down)	Lay	Write	Wrote

International English Olympiad –

Practice Exercise

Complete the sentence choosing the correct verb:

1. I am not sure what to wear/wore today in the evening.

2. Last evening, we were all standing on the pavement when a remote- controlled car flew/fly past us!

3. Can you please write/wrote an email to Sarah telling her about our plan?

4. Amit spent/spend a lot of money last month on his Europe vacation.

5. Natasha assured me that she will sent/send the uniforms today.

6. Aditya had already left/leave by the time we reached last night.

7. I am a big fan of this game. I will buy/bought it on the day it releases!

8. The accountant got/get irritated last time because we did not have all the papers.

9. My mother had told/tell me about the event last night but I forgot!

10. They always come /came to the station half an hour before the train leaves.

11. He hit/hitted the dog brutally last evening.

12. Priya drank/drink her medicine before going to sleep last night.

13. She ran/run to the garden as soon as she heard her father's footsteps.

14. I have read/readed all the Harry Potter books.

15. He was/is not in his room when I checked this morning.

Choose the correct option to fill in the blanks:

If I ask him the answer tomorrow, will he _____
- (a) fly
- (b) run
- (c) sow
- (d) know

When he picked up the stick from the ground, it was badly _____
- (a) write
- (b) buy
- (c) bent
- (d) caught

3. As soon as I went near the little bird, it _____ away.
- (a) flew
- (b) drew
- (c) sew
- (d) drank

4. 'Where are you? We are all waiting for you to _____ the cake.'
- (a) lay
- (b) lent
- (c) cut
- (d) read

5. Where should I apply if I have _____ my ID?
- (a) brought
- (b) sent
- (c) caught
- (d) lost

6. I have just _____ my old car.
- (a) told
- (b) sold
- (c) mould
- (d) fold

7. I know Mr. Mukherjee, he _____ my son last year.
- (a) flew
- (b) sent
- (c) taught
- (d) brought

8. I will meet Aman today. I _____ Suruchi yesterday.
- (a) set
- (b) read
- (c) leapt
- (d) met

9. Mansi _____ a beautiful song at the function last week.
- (a) drank
- (b) sang
- (c) rang
- (d) sank

10. I didn't know that she _____ her things when she came yesterday.
- (a) took
- (b) drank
- (c) sang
- (d) flew

11. She repeated the lesson and asked if we _____ it.
- (a) sank
- (b) brought
- (c) understood
- (d) caught

12. It was a pleasant day so we all _____ to the beach yesterday.
- (a) ran
- (b) buy
- (c) wrote
- (d) went

13. Last year when I _____ the Taj, I _____ it was beautiful. I still do.
    (a) went, thought
    (b) thought, drank
    (c) saw, thought
    (d) wrote, bought

14. Neha _____ a pink dress for her wedding.

    (a) spent
    (c) thought

    (b) wore
    (d) read

15. We all _____ up when we saw the teacher entering the classroom.
    (a) spent
    (b) wrote
    (c) stood
    (d) brought

Adverbs

9

An adverb is *a word which tells us more about another* word such as a verb, an adjective, *a clause or* even another adverb. See the examples below:

An adverb modifying a verb: He walks *slowly.*

An adverb modifying an adjective: She is *very* happy.

An adverb modifying another adverb: He walks *very* slowly.

There are different kinds of adverbs. Some of the common ones are:

Adverb of Time

These are words which give us information about when an event or action has happened. These are usually used either at the beginning or at the end of a sentence. These include words like immediately, soon, tomorrow, already, daily, often, before, yet, still, etc.

We will meet her *soon.*

Roshni eats here *often.*

Amit has worked here *before.*

Adverb of Place

These are words which give us information about where an event or action has taken place. These are mostly used after the verb. These include words like here, somewhere, below, under, inside, above, etc.

We have been *here* before.

The puppy was sitting *inside* the dog-house.

Adverb of Manner

These are words which give us information about the manner in which something has been done. A lot of these adverbs end with *the suffix – ly.* These include words like beautifully, clumsily, happily, sadly, quickly, slowly, etc.

Amita *sadly* shook my hand.

The game is *quickly* becoming popular.

Adverb of Degree

These are the words which give us information about *the intensity or the level of the action.* These include words like so, very, too, much, nearly, really, etc.

My grandfather was *too* excited to be able to sit down.

It was just the two of us but we *nearly* finished the large pizza.

Adverb of Frequency

These are words which give us information about how many times an action takes place. These include words like always, never, often, sometimes, rarely, thrice, annually, etc.

We *never* go to Shimla without him.

That book is *rarely* available.

Practice Exercise

I. Chose the correct option from the given options:

1. We meet _____ Sunday to play cricket in the stadium.
   - (a) soon
   - (b) every
   - (c) twice
   - (d) quickly

2. Tanya comes to meet me _____
   - (a) slowly
   - (b) clumsily
   - (c) often
   - (d) ago

3. It started raining, so every one moved _____
   - (a) above
   - (b) somewhere
   - (c) closely
   - (d) inside

4. She eats _____ quickly. It is not healthy.
   - (a) often
   - (b) clearly
   - (c) too
   - (d) here

5. When Amit heard about the accident, he came _____
   - (a) nearly
   - (b) u
   - (c) often
   - (d) immediately

6. Mother knocked on the door at 1 pm. They were _____ sleeping!
   - (a) quietly
   - (b) still
   - (c) very
   - (d) too

7. We came to the function even last year. It is organized _____
   - (a) annually
   - (b) quickly
   - (c) always
   - (d) slowly

8. Have you kept my watch _____? I am not able to find it!
   - (a) always
   - (b) often
   - (c) somewhere
   - (d) here

9. Rohit is very religious. He prays _____.
   - (a) rarely
   - (b) daily
   - (c) above
   - (d) quickly

10. I am not surprised that she won the scholarship. She is _____ intelligent.
    - (a) beautifully
    - (b) nearly
    - (c) sadly
    - (d) so

11. _____ cross the road from the zebra crossing.
    - (a) Always
    - (b) Here
    - (c) Beside
    - (d) Often

12. I have been sitting near the phone all day! He hasn't called _____.
    - (a) below
    - (b) often
    - (c) yet
    - (d) already

13. She painted the scene _____. I am speechless!
    - (a) restlessly
    - (b) beautifully
    - (c) often
    - (d) here

14. My grandmother has been ill for the last three months, so we go to meet her _____.
    - (a) under
    - (b) happily
    - (c) often
    - (d) never

15. The weather was great _____. We played in the park all day.
    - (a) yesterday
    - (b) often
    - (c) intently
    - (d) too

16. The class was _____ full, so we started the lecture.
    - (a) twice
    - (b) above
    - (c) quietly
    - (d) nearly

17. I have already watched this movie once but I don't mind watching it _____.
    - (a) inside
    - (b) again
    - (c) always
    - (d) soon

18. Nisha is a good dancer. She practices _____
    - (a) really
    - (b) often
    - (c) everyday
    - (d) sometimes

19. Put the cat _____ the blanket.
    - (a) under
    - (b) below
    - (c) again
    - (d) yet

20. I asked her if she had visited the Red Fort _____ but she told me that this was her first visit.
    - (a) after
    - (b) inside
    - (c) before
    - (d) tomorrow

II. Choose the correct answer from the options given in the sentence.

1. We are busy with school today. We can come and visit you guys slowly/tomorrow.

2. Shahrukh has rarely/always been my favourite actor.

3. When I heard Ashish singing, I was really/poorly impressed.

4. The teacher asked Rahul to sit down and he rarely/obediently sat down.

5. When I asked her to join me for lunch, she happily/already accepted.

6. I sometimes/much like to go for a jog in the morning.

7. When he delivered my things, I asked him to keep them on/much the table.

8. By the time Anita reached the theatre, the movie had already/rarely begun.

9. The doctor advised her to take the medicine twice/inside a day.

10. They spent Sunday lazily/slowly watching TV.

Adjectives

A word that describes a noun or a pronoun is called adjective. Adjectives are the words that modify another person or thing in the sentence.

For example:

(i)   Rita is a *beautiful* girl.

(Here, the word 'beautiful' describes the noun 'Rita'. So, beautiful is the adjective.

(ii) Utsav is wearing a *black* shirt.

Here, the colour of the shirt is described as black. So, black is the adjective.

Types of Adjectives

Adjective of Quality

When a noun or a pronoun is described as 'of what kind,' the describing word is called adjective of quality.

For example:

(i)   Divanshi is carrying a *blue* bag.

(Here, the bag is described as blue. So, blue is the adjective.)

(ii) Rytham is an *intelligent* student.

(Here, Rytham is described as intelligent. So, intelligent is the adjective.)

Adjective of Quantity

When the noun or the pronoun is described as 'how many' or 'how much,' the describing word is called adjective of quantity.

For example:

(i)   Ajay has three chocolates.

(Here, three is describing the number of chocolates. So, three is the adjective.)

(ii) We have sufficient space to park our car.

(Here, sufficient describes the space. So, sufficient is the adjective.)

Degrees of Adjectives

There are three degrees of adjectives.

(i)   Positive

(ii) Comparative

(iii) Superlative

These degrees of comparison help us to describe things more clearly and accurately.

For example:

Positive	Comparative	Superlative
Big	Bigger	Biggest
Tall	Taller	Tallest
Much	More	Most
Small	Smaller	Smallest
Few	Fewer	Fewest
Little/Less	Lesser	Least
Fine	Finer	Finest
Beautiful	More beautiful	Most beautiful

Practice Exercise

I. Fill in the blanks with the correct option.

1. Sonia is wearing a _____ dress.
   - (a) beautiful
   - (b) tall
   - (c) thin
   - (d) none of these

2. The Taj Mahal is of _____ colour.
   - (a) grey
   - (b) black
   - (c) yellow
   - (d) white

3. Her school bag is _____.
   - (a) pure
   - (b) fake
   - (c) new
   - (d) nothing

4. It was a _____ day.
   - (a) sunny
   - (b) jealous
   - (c) cruel
   - (d) white

5. We like to sit under _____ stars.
   - (a) orange
   - (b) bright
   - (c) funny
   - (d) soft

6. Can I play with your _____ toy?
   - (a) new
   - (b) brave
   - (c) exhausted
   - (d) stale

7. The elephant is _____ than the cow.
   - (a) biggest
   - (b) big
   - (c) more big
   - (d) bigger

8. Do you have _____ labour?
   - (a) ten
   - (b) clever
   - (c) sufficient
   - (d) blue

9. Mr. Kapoor is a _____ person
   - (a) humble
   - (b) two
   - (c) some
   - (d) whole

II. Choose the correct option and fill in the blanks.

1. Do you drink _____ water?
   - (a) clean
   - (b) tasty
   - (c) wise
   - (d) pink

2. Why are you eating _____ mangoes?
   - (a) sour
   - (b) careful
   - (c) low
   - (d) tough

3. Khali is a _____ wrestler.
   - (a) sorrow
   - (b) indian
   - (c) tough
   - (d) interesting

4. It was a _____ scene.
   - (a) tall
   - (b) black
   - (c) major
   - (d) beautiful

5. These cats are of _____ colours.
   - (a) each
   - (b) brown and white
   - (c) all
   - (d) none of these

6. My friend was sitting in the _____ row.
   - (a) fifth
   - (b) deep
   - (c) bright
   - (d) many

7. The entire area was _____
   - (a) bright
   - (b) peaceful
   - (c) powerful
   - (d) tender

8. They are _____ swimmers.
   - (a) high
   - (b) low
   - (c) bright
   - (d) good

9. My new cricket kit is the _____ gift from my parents.
   - (a) most wonderful
   - (b) wonder fullest
   - (c) more wonderful
   - (d) wonderful

10. Manak is the _____ kid in the class.
    - (a) funny
    - (b) more funny
    - (c) funnier
    - (d) funniest

◆◆◆

Articles

11

The English alphabet comprises of vowels and consonants. The letters a, e, i, o and u are vowels. The rest of the letters are consonants.

There are three articles in English: *a, an* and *the*. *A* and *an* are indefinite articles and *the* is a definite article.

Indefinite article

Indefinite refers to uncertainty. Indefinite articles refer to something that is 'general' or uncertain. When we talk about any one thing in general, we use the indefinite articles *a* or *an*.

We use *a* before a word that starts with a consonant sound. Always make sure that you focus on the sound of the letters instead of the letters themselves. Pay attention to the pronunciation of the words.

a useful advice (it begins with 'yoo' sound which is a consonant)

Examples: a window, a horse, a girl, a uniform (it begins with 'yoo' sound which is a consonant)

Note: We use 'an' before a word that starts with a vowel sound.

Examples: an orange, an owl, an orange tree, an ice cream, an aeroplane,

an honest man ('h' is silent, so the word begins with 'o', which is a vowel)

Definite article

Definite refers to be sure or certain about a thing. It means that we are talking about a specific thing or event. In such cases, we use the definite article 'the'.

We use *a* when we talk about something for the first time. We use *the* when we talk about the same thing again.

Example:

I am wearing *a* red sweater. *The* sweater is too big for me.

In the first sentence, we do not know which sweater we are talking about, so we use the indefinite article *a*. In the second sentence, we know which sweater we are talking about, so we use the definite article *the*.

We also use *the* before the following:

(i) names of mountain ranges, famous monuments, the names of seas, rivers, and religious books, etc.

(ii) the superlative degrees of adjective

(iii) the names of heavenly bodies

Examples: The Eiffel Tower, The Ganges, The Himalayas, The Holy Koran, The Earth, The tallest building.

We do not use the article *the* at some places. These are as follows:

(i) before the names of festivals: Diwali, Christmas, and Eid

(ii) before the names of games: football, cricket, volleyball

(iii) before the names of languages: French, German, Spanish

(iv) before proper nouns and abstract nouns: Mr. Smith, happiness

Practice Exercise

I. Fill in the blanks with the correct option:

1. _____ Earth is not round.
   - (a) A
   - (b) An
   - (c) The
   - (d) None

2. _____ honesty is the best policy.
   - (a) A
   - (b) An
   - (c) The
   - (d) None

3. _____ orange fell from the tree.
   - (a) A
   - (b) An
   - (c) The
   - (d) None

4. He will be back next _____ year.
   - (a) a
   - (b) an
   - (c) the
   - (d) none

5. He is _____ fastest runner in the team.
   - (a) a
   - (b) an
   - (c) the
   - (d) none

6. I need _____ pen. Do you have one?
   - (a) a
   - (b) an
   - (c) the
   - (d) none

7. _____ Daksh is living in Mumbai.
   - (a) A
   - (b) An
   - (c) The
   - (d) None

8. A river flows by my house in the hills. _____ river is magnificent.
   - (a) A
   - (b) An
   - (c) The
   - (d) None

9. Do you need _____ umbrella?
   - (a) a
   - (b) an
   - (c) the
   - (d) none

10. Have you read _____ Bhagvad Gita?
    - (a) a
    - (b) an
    - (c) the
    - (d) none

11. _____ Eid is celebrated with a lot of love.
    - (a) A
    - (b) An
    - (c) The
    - (d) None

12. He offered me _____ apple to eat.
    - (a) a
    - (b) an
    - (c) the
    - (d) none

13. Have you ever seen _____ ostrich?
    - (a) a
    - (b) an
    - (c) the
    - (d) none

14. _____ volcano is located in the eastern corner of _____ city.
    - (a) A, the
    - (b) An, a
    - (c) The, the
    - (d) The, a

15. My mother is having _____ headache.
    - (a) a
    - (b) an
    - (c) the
    - (d) none

II. Complete the following:

1. _____ easy task
   - (a) A
   - (b) An
   - (c) The
   - (d) None

2. _____ longest jump
   - (a) A
   - (b) An
   - (c) The
   - (d) None

3. _____ unhappy unicorn
   - (a) A
   - (b) An
   - (c) The
   - (d) None

4. _____ hour later
   - (a) A
   - (b) An
   - (c) The
   - (d) None

5. _____ steepest mountain
   - (a) A
   - (b) An
   - (c) The
   - (d) None

6. _____ owl
   - (a) A
   - (b) An
   - (c) The
   - (d) None

7. _____ new dress
   - (a) A
   - (b) An
   - (c) The
   - (d) None

8. _____ golden brick
   - (a) A
   - (b) An
   - (c) The
   - (d) None

9. _____ Taj Mahal
   - (a) A
   - (b) An
   - (c) The
   - (d) None

10. _____ Assam
    - (a) A
    - (b) An
    - (c) The
    - (d) None

11. _____ ice cream
    (a) A
    (b) An
    (c) The
    (d) None

12. _____ rotten egg
    (a) A   (b) An
    (c) The   (d) None

13. _____ house next to mine
    (a) A   (b) An
    (c) The   (d) None

14. _____ spinning top
    (a) A   (b) An
    (c) The   (d) None

15. _____ Indian Express
    (a) A   (b) An
    (c) The   (d) None

◆◆◆

A preposition is a word which helps you understand the relationship between different words in a sentence. Prepositions are usually positioned before the noun in a sentence. For example, keep the food on the table. Here *on* tells you the position of the food with reference to the table.

There are two major kinds of prepositions:

Prepositions of Place

These include all the prepositions which indicate the position or the direction of the noun. See some examples to understand them better.

'In'
This preposition is used when the area being talked about has some defined borders.

Example:

in a box

'On'
This preposition is used when referring to the outer surface of something.

Example:

on the blackboard

'Under'
This preposition is used when referring to a position lower than or underneath something.

Example:

under the bridge

'Below'
This preposition is used when referring to a position, which is lower in comparison to something but higher in comparison to another.

Example:

below the cover

'Over'
This preposition is used when referring to an object covering another.

Example:

Put the blanket over the baby.

It is also used when referring to an action of getting 'across' something.

Example:

Walking over the bridge.

'Above'
This preposition is used when referring to a position, which is higher than something else but not directly 'on' it.

Example:

I live in the flat above.

'Across'
This preposition is used when referring to the action of getting to the other side. Example:

She went to the shop *across* the street.

'Through'
This preposition is used while referring to something which has limitations and size. Example:

They drove *through* the tunnel

'Into'
This preposition is used while referring to a movement towards the inside of something.

Example:

Raman jumped into the pool.

She came into the room.

'At'
This preposition is used when referring to an exact location or place.

Example:

at the door of the room

at the corner of the street

'To'
This preposition is used to indicate direction and consequence of motion.

Example:

to the school

to the Principal

'Towards'

This preposition is also used to indicate the direction of restaurant.

Example:

towards the food

'From'

This preposition is used to indicate where the 'object' or person is coming from.

Example:

This cake is from the nearby bakery.

She hails from Himachal Pradesh.

Prepositions of time

These prepositions are used to indicate the time when an event takes place. See the examples to understand them better

'From'

This preposition is used to indicate the time when an event begins.

Example:

We heard the song *from* noon till evening.

'By'

This preposition is used to indicate the latest/outer limit of some event.

Example:

We have to reach his place latest *by* 6 or we will not be able to meet him.

'On'

This preposition is used to indicate the exact date when an event takes place.

Example:

My uncle is returning from Dubai on the 7th.

'At'

This preposition is used to indicate the tim broadly when an event takes place.

Example:

We go for a walk *at* night.

'Ago'

This preposition is used to indicate a specific tim in the past.

Example:

I met Neha again two days *ago*.

'Since'

This preposition is used to indicate the time peric from certain events in the past till the prese moment.

Example:

I haven't called Anand *since* last Friday.

'For'

This preposition is used to indicate the tim duration for which a certain event lasts continues.

Example:

We will be on vacation *for* three days.

'Before'

This preposition is used to indicate that an eve happened prior to another event.

Example:

We met her once *before* we came to Delhi.

'From-Till'

This set of prepositions is used to tell the durati of an event.

Example:

We walked on the beach *from* morning *till* evenin

Practice Exercise

I. **Choose the most suitable preposition to fill in the blanks:**

1. Shipra placed the chocolates _____ her bag.
   (a) Across   (b) In
   (c) To   (d) Towards

2. Please finish the work _____ 5 pm.
   (a) Of   (b) In
   (c) By   (d) On

3. Anita is sitting _____ the room.
   (a) In   (b) Of
   (c) By   (d) Since

4. Can you swim _____ the river?
   (a) Below   (b) Till
   (c) Towards   (d) Across

5. She was watching the movie _____ 4 am _____ the morning.
   (a) Of, below
   (b) Since, to
   (c) Till, in
   (d) Across, till

6. I met him two days _____ at the park.
   (a) In   (b) Towards
   (c) Ago   (d) Below

7. I will meet you _____ the McDonald's outlet _____ 7 pm today.
   (a) In, below   (b) At, above
   (c) Across, at   (d) At, At

8. We all went to that school _____ 2010.
   (a) Till   (b) By
   (c) Below   (d) Ago

9. The little puppy was hiding _____ the car.
   (a) Across   (b) Till
   (c) At   (d) Under

10. When I saw her at the mall, I waved at her and she started walking _____ me.
    (a) At   (b) Towards
    (c) By   (d) Below

11. We watched the movie _____ the living room.
    (a) Across   (b) By
    (c) Till   (d) In

12. I have not met my aunt _____ last Tuesday.
    (a) Since   (b) Till
    (c) By   (d) Ago

13. We need to be _____ the theatre by 3 p.m. or we will miss the movie.
    (a) Till   (b) By
    (c) At   (d) Since

14. Rohit came to Delhi _____ the 15th of this month.
    (a) On   (b) At
    (c) By   (d) From

15. They were on the beach _____ 12 pm _____ 6 pm.
    (a) By, till   (b) To, from
    (c) Across, by   (d) From, till

16. He is staying with us at least _____ Tuesday.
    (a) Till   (b) By
    (c) To   (d) Below

17. I waited for him for about half an hour _____ the staircase.
    (a) Across   (b) Below
    (c) Under   (d) From

18. Astha's sister is getting married _____ the 27th of November.
    (a) By   (b) Till
    (c) At   (d) On

19. She came to visit me 5 days _____.
    (a) Since   (b) By
    (c) Ago   (d) In

20. Can you please put the toys back _____ the box?
    (a) Till   (b) Across
    (c) Into   (d) To

21. I am going _____ Mumbai in August.
    (a) in   (b) to
    (c) by   (d) towards

22. The train is _____ the station.
    (a) by   (b) on
    (c) at   (d) up

23. The dog is _____ the table.
    (a) into   (b) with
    (c) at   (d) under

24. Sheehan jumped _____ the river and swam very fast.
    (a) to   (b) far
    (c) over   (d) into

25. Will you come to my house _____ Saturday?
    (a) to   (b) on
    (c) at   (d) in

26. He is working _____ the factory.
    (a) to   (b) into
    (c) in   (d) at

27. Piyu is standing _____ the tree.
    (a) under   (b) over
    (c) above   (d) up

28. I will finish the work _____ an hour.
    (a) to   (b) in
    (c) on   (d) up

29. Why is she standing in the middle _____ the road?
    (a) above   (b) beside
    (c) of   (d) near

30. Suze is sitting _____ Rhea and Upasna.
    (a) between   (b) at
    (c) until   (d) since

31. What is the time _____ your watch?
    (a) in   (b) by
    (c) at   (d) with

32. Come _____ me to Munnar.
    (a) by   (b) with
    (c) near   (d) towards

33. The plane is flying _____ the hills.
    (a) over   (b) under
    (c) towards   (d) at

34. The temperature at night is _____ 20 degree Celsius.
    (a) in   (b) below
    (c) with   (d) until

35. The crayons are _____ the box.
    (a) to   (b) at
    (c) with   (d) in

II. **Choose the correct preposition from the given alternatives in the question:**

1. Amit jogs in/at the park every morning.
2. Neha works as a teacher over/in a school.
3. My mother will be at home ago/by 3 pm.
4. We met at the mall 2 days in/ago.
5. My cat always sleeps at/in his box.
6. Tanya finishes her homework by/to 7 p.m. every evening.
7. The circus will be in town to/till the 15th.
8. She saw me through/from the binoculars.
9. Mohit always kept a first aid box on/in his car.
10. We enjoy eating at/till the Indian restaurant nearby.

III. **Choose which of the following option usage of prepositions is correct:**

(Note: 'T' stands for 'True' and 'F' stands for 'False'.)

1. I wake up at five o'clock.
   I have been awake since six o'clock.
   (a) TT   (b) FF
   (c) TF   (d) FT

2. The table is made by wood.
   The book is at the table.
   (a) TT   (b) FF
   (c) TF   (d) FT

3. The guests are at the door.
   I play with a racquet.
   (a) TT   (b) FF
   (c) TF   (d) FT

4. I am going to the shop.
   I have brought a skirt for you.
   (a) TT   (b) FF
   (c) TF   (d) FT

5. The apples grow on the tree.
   The dog was playing with a frisbee.
   (a) TT   (b) FF
   (c) TF   (d) FT

6. The interview is inside the building.
   January comes after February.
   (a) TT   (b) FF
   (c) TF   (d) FT

7. This is the story about a young man from Arabia.

   Can you come and live with us?
   (a) TT   (b) FF
   (c) TF   (d) FT

8. Delhi is the capital of India.

   We will play in the field.
   (a) TT   (b) FF
   (c) TF   (d) FT

9. Shawn is talking to Smith.

   The cattle graze in the field.
   (a) TT   (b) FF
   (c) TF   (d) FT

10. There are five girls in the team.

    There are ten boys at the team.
    (a) TT   (b) FF
    (c) TF   (d) FT

11. Jack and Jill went up the hill.

    Fruits grow on trees.

    (a) TT   (b) FF
    (c) TF   (d) FT

12. Put the vase on the floor.

    Add sugar to the tea.
    (a) TT   (b) FF
    (c) TF   (d) FT

13. The amusement park was opened for the children.

    His parents are from Ajmer.
    (a) TT   (b) FF
    (c) TF   (d) FT

14. I was born on 27th August 2000.

    I will travel by car.
    (a) TT   (b) FF
    (c) TF   (d) FT

15. The final match was played between India and Sri Lanka.

    I found a purse on the road.
    (a) TT   (b) FF
    (c) TF   (d) FT

Conjunctions

A conjunction is a word that is used to combine words or sentences together. The most common conjunctions are: and, *but, or, so, because, etc.*

And

'And' is used to combine two words or sentences of similar rank together.

Example:

I am tall and smart.

Go and bring my clothes back.

But

'But' is used to combine two conflicting or opposing ideas together.

Example:

It's easy but lengthy.

Sonia bought three pencils but she lost two of them.

Or

'Or' is used to combine two alternative options together.

Example:

I want to buy a pink or an orange dress.

Do you like reading or watching movies?

So

'So' is used to say that the second idea is the result of the first.

Example:

I am very tired so I will come with you.

It is cold and windy so we are staying at home.

Because

'Because' is used to explain the reason of something.

Example:

Because I am very tired, I will not come with you.

We are staying at home because it is raining outside.

Practice Exercise

1. I like to eat bananas _____ not oranges.
   - (a) but
   - (b) and
   - (c) or
   - (d) so

2. I need a pen _____ a piece of paper to write.
   - (a) or
   - (b) and
   - (c) but
   - (d) so

3. We have a cat ____ we do not have a dog.
   - (a) but
   - (b) and
   - (c) or
   - (d) so

4. Tomorrow, we can go for a movie _____ to the zoo, but not both.
   - (a) and
   - (b) or
   - (c) but
   - (d) so

5. I like tomatoes, carrots _____ beans.
   - (a) and
   - (b) so
   - (c) but
   - (d) or

6. We can either buy a shirt _____ a T-shirt for his birthday.
   - (a) and
   - (b) but
   - (c) or
   - (d) so

7. The elephant has long ears _____ a short tail.
   - (a) if
   - (b) or
   - (c) but
   - (d) and

8. I got a book _____ gave it to my sister.
   - (a) than
   - (b) so
   - (c) and
   - (d) but

9. Is that dress blue ____ pink?
   - (a) for
   - (b) but
   - (c) and
   - (d) or

10. We won the match _____ we played well.
    - (a) because
    - (b) if
    - (c) but
    - (d) so

11. My grandfather likes summer _____ hates winter.
    - (a) if
    - (b) but
    - (c) because
    - (d) or

12. A parrot can talk ____ it cannot draw.
    - (a) and
    - (b) but
    - (c) or
    - (d) because

13. A hen eats grains _____ worms.
    - (a) and
    - (b) but
    - (c) or
    - (d) as

14. We were tired _____ we could not read.
    - (a) because
    - (b) and
    - (c) so
    - (d) of

15. It has been a long time _____ we saw him.
    - (a) before
    - (b) since
    - (c) because
    - (d) as

16. She is intelligent _____ lazy.
    - (a) and
    - (b) but
    - (c) so
    - (d) or

17. ____ in Baroda, he learnt painting.
    - (a) Since
    - (b) While
    - (c) As
    - (d) Because

18. Do it now _____ you forget.
    - (a) or
    - (b) and
    - (c) before
    - (d) since

19. Why is he dressed _____ a woman?
    - (a) before
    - (b) after
    - (c) as
    - (d) if

20. Will you have a mango shake _____ banana shake?
    - (a) and
    - (b) if
    - (c) or
    - (d) because

Simple Tenses

14

Tenses indicate the time of action mentioned in the sentence. It is the change in the verb to show what time the action has taken place.

There are three kinds of basic tenses:

Present Tense

This tense talks about an action, which is taking place at the time of mentioning. Simple present tense is also employed while talking about universal truths, things and events, which are always true.

Example:

The Sun rises in the east.

Here the verb *rises* is in the simple present tense, because the Sun has always and will always rise from the east.

Past Tense

This tense talks about an action or events, which have already taken place or have already been completed at the time of mention.

Example:

Manu ate the chocolate yesterday.

Here, we have used past tense because the action (Manu eating the chocolate) has already been completed by the time we talk about it.

It is easy to convert a verb into its past tense form. For regular verbs, just add '–d' or '-ed' to the verb.

Example:

Ask (present tense) + ed – asked

Bake (present tense) + d – baked

Future Tense

This tense talks about events or actions, which are going to happen after the time of speaking about them. These events have not happened yet.

Example:

Srishti will go to the mall tomorrow.

Here, we have used the future tense because Srishti will go to the mall the day after she is talking about it.

For most verbs, adding the helping verb 'will' changes the verb from present tense to future tense.

Examples:

I go to buy milk every morning. (present)

I will go to buy milk tomorrow morning (future).

Tip: You can understand that the future tense is used with words like tomorrow, next week, again, some day, etc.

Practice Exercise

I. Change the verb given in brackets into the correct form.

1. Every afternoon I (go) _____ to the park.

2. It does (not/rain) _____ here a lot.

3. We (see) _____ some beautiful gardens in Jaipur last month.

4. I like to (eat) _____ at Chinese restaurants.

5. Ashley (see) _____ this movie with me tomorrow.

6. The colour of this jacket (be) _____ absolutely fine.

7. Mother (leave) _____ her shawl here when she left last week.

8. Next week I (go) _____ to Shimla on holiday.

9. This park is best to (play) _____ in the evenings.

10. I think she liked the cake. She (eat) _____ at least half of it!

11. Amit (drive) _____ his car last night.

12. Preeti and Sabina always (drink) _____ tea. They are not fond of coffee.

13. Last Friday, her father (come) _____ to drop her to the airport.

14. He _____ (not/like) the food at the party two days ago.

15. Why don't you guys go ahead. I (late) _____ by another half an hour.

II. Choose the correct option from the ones given below.

1. I _____ the video game all evening yesterday.
   (a) playing   (b) will play
   (c) played   (d) play

2. I _____ the taste of orange drink. I never drink it.
   (a) hate   (b) hated
   (c) will hate   (d) hating

3. Amrit _____ something special. His mother is coming to visit him tonight.
   (a) cooked   (b) cooking
   (c) will cook   (d) cook

4. It's his birthday tomorrow, we _____ at 12 at night.
   (a) meeting   (b) met
   (c) meets   (d) will meet

5. The movie we _____ yesterday was too funny!
   (a) will watch
   (b) watched
   (c) watch
   (d) watching

6. She is very quick on the computer. She _____ this document in just half an hour once she reaches here.
   (a) type
   (b) typing
   (c) will type
   (d) has been typing

7. India _____ Pakistan by 150 runs last week.
   (a) defeats
   (b) will defeat
   (c) have been defeating
   (d) defeated

8. As a habit, she still _____ up every morning at 5 to go for a run.
   (a) waking   (b) wakes
   (c) woken   (d) wake

9. The hero in the movie always knows how to _____ and dance.
   (a) sings   (b) sang
   (c) singing   (d) sing

10. I _____ for you for only ten minutes more. Then I will leave.
    (a) will wait   (b) waited
    (c) waits   (d) waiting

11. Ashish _____ how to use this software vey well. He does it all the time.
    (a) knowing   (b) knows
    (c) know   (d) will know

12. Last Thursday, we _____ out for ice cream.
    (a) go   (b) going
    (c) went   (d) will go

13. His phone is out of reach but I _____ once again.
    (a) trying   (b) try
    (c) tried   (d) will try

14. I _____ her if she wanted some more water but she said no.
    (a) ask   (b) asked
    (c) will ask   (d) asking

15. Nowadays, we _____ this programme on TV every night.
    (a) watch   (b) watching
    (c) watched   (d) will watch

Punctuation

Punctuations are used to create a sense of clarity and stress in sentences. It is a series of symbols used in the middle and at the end of a sentence. There are fourteen forms of punctuation in the English language. These forms are:

1.	Comma	,
2.	Period	.
3.	Colon	:
4.	Semicolon	;
5.	Quotation Mark	,,
6.	Exclamation Mark	!
7.	Question Mark	?
8.	Brackets	[] ()
9.	Ellipse or Ellipsis	..
10.	Braces	{}
11.	Hyphen	-
12.	Dash	-
13.	Apostrophe	,
14.	Parentheses	()

The following are some punctuation marks which are most commonly used:

Full Stop

Full stop is used to put an end to a declarative, imperative or negative sentence.

Examples:

John is the best student of the class.

The moon shines at night.

Comma

A comma informs the reader to pause before continuing the sentence. Unlike a period, the sentence is not over but simply being paused for a moment.

Examples:

I bought bread, butter, eggs and milk from the market.

The students from Science, Commerce and Arts streams have to attend the seminar.

Question Mark

A question mark is applied to put up a question before the audience. The question mark turns the sentence into a question rather than a statement.

Examples:

What are you doing?

Can I take your notebook?

Exclamation Mark

An exclamation mark also ends a sentence like a full stop, but the sentence is turned into an exclamation (strong feeling) rather than a simple statement.

Examples:

Bravo! We have won the match.

Alas! His dog is dead.

Semicolon

A semicolon connects two free-standing but related sentences where the conjunction has been left out. Semicolons are typically used before introduction words, such as, namely, however, therefore, that is, for example, or for instance.

Examples:

She came late; therefore, she was punished

I went to his house; but he did not welcome me.

Colon

A colon is used after a word(s) or sentence to expand or explain it. Colons are often used before listing items.

Examples:

Noun: The name of a person, place or thing is called Noun.

I will not eat this bread: it is stale.

Our Principal is a man of words: every member of the staff respects him.

Dash

It is used to indicate an abrupt stop or change of thought or to resume a scattered subject.

Examples:

Friends, companions, relatives – all deserted him.

Apostrophe

An apostrophe is used in the contraction form in place of the letter that has been removed. For example: It's uses an apostrophe to replace the 'i' in 'is.' 'It's' is the contracted form of 'it is.'

Practice Exercise

Directions for Qs 1 – 20: Choose the correct option to make the given sentences grammatically correct.

1. John said, I am in a hurry and can not spare time.
    (a) Comma   (b) Colon
    (c) Inverted comma   (d) Apostrophe

2. What is the time by your watch
    (a) Full stop
    (b) Question mark
    (c) Semi colon   (d) None of the above

3. Oh what a beautiful work of art.
    (a) Question mark
    (b) Dash
    (c) Inverted comma
    (d) Exclamation mark

4. Delhi Mumbai Kolkata and Chennai are the metropolitans of India.
    (a) Colon   (b) Apostrophe
    (c) Comma   (d) Full stop

5. Can you bring me a glass of water
    (a) Exclamation mark (b) Semi colon
    (c) Comma   (d) Question mark

6. As short pause is to comma, so long pause is to _____ .
    (a) Full stop
    (b) Exclamation mark
    (c) Colon
    (d) Question mark

7. As interrogation is to question mark, so exclamation is to _____ .
    (a) Full stop
    (b) Exclamation mark
    (c) Colon
    (d) Question mark

8. As related sentences are connected with a semi colon, so sentence is expanded with a _____ .
    (a) Full stop
    (b) Exclamation mark
    (c) Colon
    (d) Question mark

9. As a sentence is ended with a full stop, so a question is ended with a ____ .

    (a) Full stop
    (b) Exclamation mark
    (c) Colon
    (d) Question mark

10. The boys are shouting
    (a) Full stop   (b) Comma
    (c) Question mark   (d) Colon

11. Do not disturb me
    (a) Full stop   (b) Comma
    (c) Question mark   (d) Colon

12. Why are you not attending the school these days
    (a) Full stop   (b) Comma
    (c) Question mark   (d) Colon

13. Meena Usha and Rekha are real sisters.
    (a) Comma
    (b) Question mark
    (c) Colon
    (d) Exclamation mark

14. Keep silence please
    (a) Question mark   (b) Full stop
    (c) Comma   (d) Colon

15. Work hard otherwise you will get low marks
    (a) Semi-colon   (b) Question mark
    (c) Full stop   (d) Comma

16. Do not commit any crime God is watching you.
    (a) Semi-colon
    (b) Question mark
    (c) Colon
    (d) Exclamation mark

17. No she has stolen my pen.
    (a) Comma   (b) Apostrophe
    (c) Exclamation mark (d) Full stop

18. I am quite well thank you.
    (a) Comma   (b) Full stop
    (c) Exclamation mark (d) Colon

19. Alas he died.
    (a) Full stop
    (b) Exclamation mark
    (c) Comma
    (d) Question mark

SECTION 2
READING
COMPREHENSION

Tips on Reading Comprehension

Reading will help you understand the world around you in a better way. It is like an exercise for the mind. In this day of fast internet, there is a lot of information that you will come across every day. You will need to find out which information is helpful and which one is not. This is why you should practise reading various text types like stories, short dialogues, etc., which will help you acquire a broad understanding of various texts and look for specific information in short texts like messages, invitations, etc.

Tips for improving reading comprehension skills

The following are some tips that can help you improve your reading comprehension skills:

1. **Read the text aloud and at least twice:** When you read the text aloud, you get more time to understand the information. Also, it is important to read the text slowly at first so that you get a grasp of what is given in the text. Reading the text more than once will always help make things clearer.

2. **Read a lot of books:** You should read as much as you can. Read the books that are not too hard. It will help you understand the contents of several tests or lessons.

3. **Always keep a dictionary handy:** Buy a pocket dictionary, or keep a dictionary handy. Consult it when you are unable to find the meaning of a word. However, you do not need to keep looking up all difficult words in the dictionary. Sometimes, it helps just to guess the meaning from the context.

4. **Improve vocabulary:** Having a good vocabulary can help you gain an advantage when you are reading. Build a solid foundation when it comes to words.

Solved Examples

Comprehension 1

Read the passage below and answer the questions that follow:

The Enormous Turnip

Ali's grandfather planted six turnip seeds and watered them daily. All the turnips grew, but there was one turnip that grew bigger than the other turnips. It wasn't just big. It was ENORMOUS! Ali's grandfather tried to pull the turnip out. He pulled and pulled, but could not pull the turnip out. So, Ali's grandfather called Ali's grandmother to help pull the turnip out. They pulled and pulled, but could not pull the turnip out. Then they called Ali's sister to help them pull the turnip out. They pulled and pulled and pulled, but could not pull the turnip out. Finally, Ali said, 'I am coming. I will help you all in pulling the turnip out' He joined the chain. They pulled and pulled and pulled and pulled, and POP! Out came the turnip.

1. What did Ali's grandfather plant?

   Ans: Ali's grandfather planted turnip seeds.

2. Which turnip did Ali's grandfather try to pull out?

   Ans: Ali's grandfather tried to pull out the enormous turnip.

3. Who did Ali's grandfather call first to pull the turnip out?

   Ans: Ali's grandfather called Ali's grandmother first to pull the turnip out.

4. Fill in the blanks.
   a. Ali's grandparents called <u>Ali's sister</u> to help them in pulling the turnip out.
   b. Ali was the <u>last person</u> to join the chain.

5. What happened when Ali joined the chain?

   Ans: When Ali joined the chain, the turnip came out.

Comprehension 2

Read the passage below and answer the questions that follow.

The Goblin's Mushroom

Dia was looking for a goblin's mushroom. Her mother had told her a goblin story yesterday and she knew that goblins lived under mushrooms. But she lived with the fairies. And the fairies were not allowed to talk to the goblins. Goblins were mischievous. They were always playing pranks on the fairies. But Dia wanted the mushroom for its magical power. It was easy to find one, if she knew a goblin. Some of them had poison also. So, one day Dia waited at the fairy pond to find a goblin. After waiting for two fairy days, she found a goblin that had come to drink the water of the pond.

Dia followed the goblin to the mushroom. It was so big and looked like an umbrella. Dia was about to pull it out when the goblin looked up at her. He said, 'You look like a kind fairy. Why are you taking away my home?' Dia realized she had been going to do the wrong thing. She smiled at the goblin and said, 'Thank you. I just came to meet you. I was looking for you under the mushroom. You are a nice goblin.'

The goblin served Dia some hot chocolate and then Dia went back to the fairies and told them about how nice the goblins were.

1. Complete the sentences.
   Ans: a. Dia was looking for a goblin's <u>mushroom</u>.
   b. Dia lived with the <u>fairies</u>.

2. Number the things that happen in the story in the right sequence.

   Ans:

a. Dia had hot chocolate with the goblin.	3
b. Dia waited at the pond.	1
c. Dia followed the goblin	2

3. Name the two magical creatures that the story talks about.

Ans: <u>Fairies and goblins</u>

4. Why were the fairies not allowed to talk to the goblins?

Ans: The fairies were not allowed to talk to the goblins because they were mischievous. They were always playing pranks on the fairies.

5. Tick the correct answer.

a. What did the goblin's mushroom look like?
   i. book
   ii. umbrella ☑
   iii. moon

b. Who said this line and to whom?

Ans: I was looking for you under the mushroom.
   i. goblin to Dia
   ii. goblin to the fairies
   iii. Dia to goblin ☑

6. What did Dia tell the fairies when she went back?

Ans: Dia told the fairies about how nice the goblins were.

Comprehension 3

Read the conversation below and answer the questions that follow:

(Aditi and Sourav meet at the sports shop.)

Aditi: Hey Sourav. What are you doing here?

Sourav: I came to buy a tennis ball for practice.

Aditi: Oh! I forgot completely. Congratulations Sourav, you won a gold medal in the inter-school tennis match.

Sourav: Thank you, Aditi. I am glad I was able to win the match. Our principal, Mrs. Ahuja and our PT teacher, Prashant Sir, called my parents to congratulate them. It was one of the happiest days of my life.

Aditi: I can imagine. You have done our school very proud. Tomorrow your name will be announced in the special assembly at the school.

Sourav: I can't wait to meet my other friends from school. I want to show them the medal.

Aditi: Yes, they all were talking about you. I am glad we met here.

Sourav: Yes, so am I. What brought you here?

Aditi: I came to buy a football. I play football with my friends every day in the park.

Sourav: I love football. Will you mind if I also came to play some time?

Aditi: Oh not at all. It would be great to have you in my team.

Sourav (smiling): Thank you, Aditi. You are a very good friend.

1. Fill in the blanks with the correct words.
   a. Aditi and Sourav met at the <u>sports</u> shop.
   b. Sourav had won a <u>gold medal</u> in the inter-school tennis match.

2. Who congratulates whom in the conversation?

Ans: Aditi congratulates Sourav in the conversation.

3. Who calls Sourav's parents?

Ans: Mrs. Ahuja, the school principal, and the PT teacher, Prashant Sir, call Sourav's parents.

4. Where will Sourav's name be announced?

Ans: Sourav's name will be announced in the special assembly at the school.

5. What does Aditi want to buy at the sports shop?

Ans: Aditi wants to buy a football from the sports shop.

Comprehension 4

Mrs. Taneja has to leave home to attend to one of her patients at the clinic. Her daughter, Ritu is not back from her swimming classes. Mrs.

Taneja decides to leave a message for Ritu so that she can take care of things for her. Read Mrs. Taneja's message and answer the questions that follow:

> **Ritu,**
> I have to leave for the clinic. I wanted to wait for you, but it was urgent. Please take our dog, Winnie, for a walk. Also, there is food for you in the refrigerator. Heat it in the microwave and then have the food. I hope you will finish the English report that is due tomorrow. I will be back around nine o'clock. Do not miss your bedtime.
> Love,
> Mom

1. How are Ritu and Mrs. Taneja related?
   Ans: Mrs. Taneja is Ritu's mom.
2. What is Mrs. Taneja's profession?
   Ans: Mrs. Taneja seems to be a doctor.
3. What is the name of their dog?
   Ans: The name of their dog is Winnie.
4. Which report does Mrs. Taneja want Ritu to finish?
   Ans: Mrs. Taneja wants Ritu to complete her English report.
5. When is Mrs. Taneja expected to return?
   Ans: Mrs. Taneja is expected to return at 9.00 p.m.

Comprehension 5

Read the invitation below and answer the questions that follow:

> The management, staff and students of
> **Bal Bharti Higher Secondary School**
> cordially invite you to their Annual Sports Day to be held on the school grounds
> at 9.00 a.m.
> on Saturday, 12th July 2019
> Mr Ashok Fernandez, the Sports Secretary of the state, will be the chief guest of honour. Prizes will be distributed at 11.00 a.m. Your presence will be a source of encouragement for the students.
> Please note
> 1) Please be seated by 8.50 a.m. sharp.
> 2) This card is valid for two persons only.

1. What is the occasion at the school?
   Ans: The school is organizing its annual sports day.
2. Where is the annual sports day organized at the school?
   Ans: The annual sports day is being held on the school grounds.
3. Who is the chief guest of honour at the sports day function?
   Ans: Mr. Ashok Fernandez, the Sports Secretary of the state, is the chief guest of honour at the sports day function.
4. When will the prizes be distributed?
   Ans: Prizes will be distributed at 11.00 a.m.
5. How many persons will be allowed to enter with one invitation card?
   Ans: Two persons will be allowed to enter with one invitation card.

Practice Exercise

Comprehension 1

Read the passage below and answer the questions that follow:

Milo is a lion cub. He was born to Mr. Khalif, the lion. Mr. Khalif is the king of the jungle. Though they live in a comfortable den in the forest, Mr. Khalif takes Milo to camp in the dense forests. He wants to raise a brave lion. Milo is very friendly with the other animals. He plays ludo with his zebra friend, Abu. Milo often says that it is very difficult to win at the game with Abu. In the evening, Mrs. Khalif bakes delicious cakes for Abu and Milo. They sometimes camp together with Mr. Khalif. Abu often tells Mr. Khalif that he is a very good king of the jungle and that all animals love him.

1. Who is Milo?

_____

2. What is the name of Milo's zebra friend?

_____

3. Why does Mr. Khalif take Milo to camp in the dense forest?

_____

4. Which game is Abu very good at playing?

_____

5. What does Mrs. Khalif do for Milo and Abu?

_____

6. What does Abu often tell Mr. Khalif?

_____

Comprehension 2

Read the passage below and answer the questions that follow:

Once there was a car called Derbie. Derbie was the fastest car in town. It had a shiny red number plate and four black wheels that went round and round the whole town. Derbie was proud of its owner, Mr. Biswas. Mr. Biswas would take Derbie to the garage every Sunday. There, the mechanic would give Derbie a good wash and change its tyres, if there was a need. Derbie is very special to Mr. Biswas as it is his first car. It is the car in which Mr. Biswas had brought his newly born son to his home.

Now Mr. Biswas has grown old. His son has also brought a new car. But Mr. Biswas still takes Derbie to the town every Sunday. It is not the fastest car now, but the oldest. Sometimes, Mr. Biswas takes Mrs. Biswas for long rides in the car and they listen to old songs. Derbie is also old, but is still very proud of its owners and is very fond of them.

1. Who is the story about?
2. What was so special about Derbie?
3. Name the owner of Derbie.
4. What did the mechanic at the garage do for Derbie?
5. Why is Derbie so special to Mr. Biswas?
6. Where does Mr. Biswas take Derbie every Sunday?

Comprehension 3

Read the conversation below and answer the questions that follow.

(Kshitij and Zaira are talking to their drama teacher, Mrs. Sen.)

Mrs. Sen: Kshitij and Zaira, I am going to give you the responsibility of selecting a play for the school morning assembly.

Kshitij: Ma'am, how many actors do we have?

Mrs. Sen: We have at least ten actors.

Zaira: My mother can write a play. She is a playwright. May I take her help?

Mrs. Sen: You may, but only if she has time.

Zaira: She has been quite busy lately. What else should we do?

Mrs. Sen: You should visit the library and look for a book that has a collection of short plays.

Kshitij: Ma'am, what kind of a play should we select?

Mrs. Sen: I think you should select a comedy. We want everybody to have a good start to their day.

Zaira: Ma'am, can we enact a scene from a movie?

Mrs. Sen: It should not be a problem, but please choose with care.

Kshitij: I have just the idea. What about a scene from the Harry Potter movie?

Mrs. Sen: That is a wonderful idea, children. I can easily arrange for the costumes too. Let me discuss this with the drama club tomorrow. Thank you for your help.

Khistij and Zaira (together): My pleasure, Ma'am.

1. Who is Mrs. Sen?
2. What responsibility does Mrs. Sen give to Kshitij and Zaira?
3. What does Zaira's mother do?
4. Why does Mrs. Sen want Kshitij and Zaira to choose a comedy?
5. Which movie does Kshitij suggest they should play a scene from?
6. Who does Mrs. Sen want to discuss the idea with?

Comprehension 4

Ashima's brother, Bharat, called to say that he would be coming by the Rajdhani Express at 7.00 p.m. He needs their father to pick him up from the station. But Ashima has to leave for her tuition classes. So, she decides to leave a message for her father, Mr. Kapoor. Read the message below and answer the questions that follow:

Dad

> Bharat called to say that he will reach the railway station around 7.00 p.m. He needs you to pick him up from the railway station. I am going for my Maths tuition class. I will be back by 7.30 p.m. The car keys are in the bottom drawer of your study desk. See you soon.
>
> Ashima

1. How are Ashima and Bharat related?
2. Why did Bharat call home?
3. Which train is Bharat coming from?
4. Where is Ashima going?
5. When will Ashima be back?
6. Where are Mr. Kapoor's car keys?

Comprehension 5

Read the invitation below and answer the questions that follow:

> Mrs. and Mr. Pablo
> would like to invite you to the
> marriage of their son
> Federick Pablo
> to
> the daughter of Mrs. and Mr. Pinto
> Sunita Pinto
> on Saturday, 22nd June 2019
> at 3.00 p.m. in the afternoon
> at the Sacred Heart Church, Mapusa, Goa
> Please join us in blessing the couple.
> RSVP

1. What is the occasion of the invitation?
2. Name the couple who is getting married
3. Whose son is getting married?
4. Whose daughter is getting married?
5. When is the marriage taking place?
6. What is the venue of the marriage?

◆◆◆

SECTION 3
SPOKEN AND WRITTEN EXPRESSIONS

Let's Speak

The most important use of language is that it helps us express our thoughts to others. It is important to be fluent in language. In order to learn a language, you should learn to think in that language. It also helps to know how to react in a particular situation.

Greeting Someone in English

It is a sign of good manners when you greet someone. You wish someone in the morning by saying, 'Good morning'. Similarly, you greet someone in the afternoon by saying, 'Good afternoon'. While greeting someone in the evening, one might say, 'Good evening'. And how do you greet someone before you go to bed? You say, 'Good night'.

When you greet someone close to you, you say, 'Hello' to them. And what will you say if someone is leaving? You say, 'Good bye'. When you know you are going to see this person some time soon, you say, 'See you soon,' or 'See you later.'

Special Greetings

When should you say?	What should you say?
On the Christmas festival	Merry Christmas/ Happy Christmas
At the beginning of a new year	Happy New Year
On someone's birthday	Happy Birthday; Many many happy returns of the day
At someone's wedding anniversary	Happy Wedding Anniversary
When someone has a good news to share with you	Congratulations
When someone has done something well	Well done
When someone is trying to do something well	Good luck
When someone is not well	Get well soon

Shaking Hands

When you meet someone in a formal situation for the first time, you shake their hands and say, 'How do you do?' or 'Nice to meet you.' But we do not shake hands with people we don't know very well.

Examples:

{Swati meets Ananya and her mother (Mrs. Verma) in the market.}

Swati:	Good morning, Ananya.
Ananya:	Good morning, Swati. How are you?
Swati:	I am fine. Thank you. How are you?
Ananya:	I am good. Swati, this is my mom. Mom, this is Swati. We are in the sports club together.
Mrs. Verma:	Nice to meet you, Swati.
Swati:	Nice to meet you, too. Do you live nearby?
Mrs. Verma:	Yes, we live right across this block.
Swati:	That is great. I come for my tuitions here. Can I visit you some time?
Mrs. Verma:	That would be really nice.
Swati:	Well, see you later Mrs. Verma. It was nice to meet you.
Mrs Verma:	Same here. See you soon.

Formal Introductions: First meeting

While introducing yourself formally, you say your name and say a little bit about yourself:

Examples:

Hello, I am Vineet Sharma. Nice to meet you.

I am Shweta. I work as a teacher.

The response to such introductions would be as follows:

Hello Vineet. I am Ashutosh Gaur. Nice to meet you too.

Hello Shweta. I am Vikas. How do you do?

While introducing others, you say a little bit about them.

Examples:

Mr. Das, may I introduce my boss Lynne Mason?

Hey Kabir, I would like you to meet my mother, Anuradha Kapoor.

Informal Meetings

When you meet someone you have already met, the person is no longer a stranger. You can ask the person about what they have been doing, or you could always talk about the weather.

Examples:

(Abhi and Simran meet at an annual conference)

Abhi: Hello Simran. How are you?

Simran: Hey Abhi. I am good. How have you been?

Abhi: Not so good. I was suffering from typhoid last month.

Simran: Good God. Are you alright now?

Abhi: Yes, I am quite well. The doctor said I recovered very well. Besides, my mom took care of me.

Simran: That's good to hear.

Abhi: So what have you been up to? I haven't heard from you in quite a while.

Simran: I have been very busy with work and kids.

Abhi: How many kids do you have?

Simran: Just one. He is turning eight tomorrow.

Abhi: Wish him a happy birthday.

Simran: Thank you. I will.

Abhi: I must leave now. My boss is calling me. It was nice to meet you again.

Simran: Pleasure is mine. See you soon.

Abhi: See you.

Thanking Someone

When someone helps you do something, you should make it a point to express your gratitude. There are many ways of thanking someone in English.

Examples:

Thank you.

Thank you very much.

I appreciate it.

How to respond to a 'thank you'?

You can return someone's expression of thanks as follows:

You are welcome.

Sure.

No problem.

Don't mention it.

It's my pleasure.

Asking for Permissions

Every now and then, you will need to ask permission from people. When you ask someone's permission to use something that belongs to them, you have to be polite. You should try to use the word 'Please' as much as possible.

Examples:

Can I switch on the fan?

May I use your phone, please?

Is it okay if I open the window?

Would it be all right if I borrowed your pen?

Giving Permission

Some of the phrases used when someone gives you permission to do something are as follows:

Yes, please do.

Sure, go ahead.

Sure.

No problem.

Please feel free.

Refusing to give permission

It is possible that someone might refuse permission to do something. Given below are some phrases used while refusing permission:

No, please don't.

I'm afraid, but you can't.

I am sorry, but please don't.

Examples:

(Arshi wants to ask her teacher's permission to skip her English test)

Arshi: Ma'am, I have a request to make.

Teacher: Yes Arshi, what is it?

Arshi: Ma'am, will it be okay if I skip the English test tomorrow? My parents are out of town and my grandmother cannot help me prepare for the test.

Teacher: Sure, you may. But I am afraid this is the last time you are allowed to do that.

Arshi: Thank you, Ma'am.

Practice Exercise

I. **Choose the correct alternative from the given options:**

1. You wish someone in the morning by saying _____
   - (a) Good evening
   - (b) Good night
   - (c) Good morning
   - (d) Good bye

2. When you greet someone close to you, you say, _____ to them.
   - (a) Here
   - (b) Hello
   - (c) Yo
   - (d) Ok

3. What do you say when someone is leaving?
   - (a) Good job
   - (b) Good work
   - (c) Good riddance
   - (d) Good bye

4. How do you wish someone on their wedding anniversary?
   - (a) Well done
   - (b) Merry wedding anniversary
   - (c) Get well soon
   - (d) Happy wedding anniversary

5. What will you say when someone shares a piece of good news with you?
   - (a) Get well soon
   - (b) Congratulations
   - (c) Happy birthday
   - (d) Happy new year

6. What will you say to a person who is not well?
   - (a) Get well soon
   - (b) Congratulations
   - (c) Happy birthday
   - (d) Happy new year

7. How will you wish someone on Christmas?
   - (a) Happy birthday
   - (b) Merry Christmas
   - (c) Happy new year
   - (d) Happy Easter

8. Which of the following is the correct response to 'How do you do?'
   - (a) Who are you?
   - (b) My name is Peter.
   - (c) Peter is very good.
   - (d) I am fine. Thank you.

9. What do you say when you introduce yourself to a person for the first time?
   - (a) Your thoughts about the weather
   - (b) Your name and a little bit about yourself
   - (c) Your address
   - (d) Your hobbies

10. Which of the following is the correct response to 'Nice to meet you'?
    - (a) You are wearing a nice scarf.
    - (b) I am fine, thank you.
    - (c) What is your name?
    - (d) Same here.

11. Which of the following expression shows gratitude?
    - (a) Congratulations
    - (b) Happy birthday
    - (c) Thank you
    - (d) Well done

12. Which of the following is a nice way of responding to a 'Thank you'?
    - (a) But why?
    - (b) Who are you?
    - (c) You are welcome.
    - (d) Really?

13. Which of the following expressions is used mostly while asking for permission?
    - (a) Please
    - (b) Sorry
    - (c) Thank you
    - (d) Well done

14. Which of the following expressions is used when someone gives you permission to do something?
    - (a) No, please don't.
    - (b) Please feel free.
    - (c) I am afraid, you can't.
    - (d) Thank you

15. Which of the following expressions is used when someone does not give you permission to do something?
    - (a) Yes, please do.
    - (b) I am afraid, you can't.
    - (c) Sure, go ahead.
    - (d) No problem.

II. **Complete the following dialogues.**

1. **(Ravi and Vinod meet at the park. Vinod is with his wife.)**

   Ravi: Hello Vinod. How are you?

   Vinod: a. _____, thank you. This is my wife, Nisha. And Nisha, this is Ravi, my colleague.

   Ravi: Hello Nisha. b. _____ .

   Nisha: Hello Ravi. Nice to meet you, too.

   Ravi: I heard you two had a baby girl. c. _____ .

Nisha and Vinod: d._____ Ravi.

Ravi: Have you chosen a name for the baby yet?

Nisha: We haven't decided yet. But we are having a ceremony for the baby tomorrow. I hope Vinod has invited you.

Ravi: Of course, I will come. I must leave now. e._____ .

Nisha and Vinod: Yes, see you soon.

2. **(Rahul and Arti are meeting for the first time.)**

Rahul: Good morning. I am a. _____.

Arti: Good morning Rahul. I am Arti. Pleased to meet you.

Rahul: b._____ too. I want to know about the book that you are writing.

Arti: It is nearly done. But I am finding it difficul[t] to conclude the book. Do you know of a good library where I can find some classics?

Rahul: Oh yes, there is a library right next to my house. c._____ give me a list of the books tha[t] you need. I will get them for you.

Arti: d._____ Rahul. I appreciate it.

Rahul: e._____, no problem.

3. **(Ritu needs her mother's permission to go to watch a movie with her friends.)**

Ritu: Mom, my friends are going to watch the new movie that has released this Friday. a._____ [I] go with them?

Mother: b. _____, you can't go. We have guests over.

Ritu: c. _____ okay if I go next weekend?

Mother: d. _____, please do.

Ritu: e. _____ so much, mom.

◆◆◆

SECTION 4
ACHIEVERS' SECTION

Higher Order Thinking Skills (HOTS)

I. Choose the kind of noun that has been underlined from the given options:

1. Ram was sitting on the <u>carpet</u>.
   - (a) Proper Noun
   - (b) Common Noun
   - (c) Abstract Noun
   - (d) Collective noun

2. Sita drove her <u>Audi</u> back home.
   - (a) Proper Noun
   - (b) Common Noun
   - (c) Abstract Noun
   - (d) Collective noun

3. <u>Fear</u> is a basic emotion.
   - (a) Proper Noun
   - (b) Concrete Noun
   - (c) Abstract Noun
   - (d) Collective noun

4. Tom saw a <u>flock</u> of birds flying in the sky.
   - (a) Proper Noun
   - (b) Common Noun
   - (c) Abstract Noun
   - (d) Collective noun

5. Jack likes playing in the <u>snow</u>.
   - (a) Proper Noun
   - (b) Uncountable Noun
   - (c) Abstract Noun
   - (d) Countable Noun

II. Fill in the blanks with the correct choice:

1. Rohan bought himself _____ vanilla ice-cream. It was _____ ice candy.
   - (a) An, A
   - (b) A, The
   - (c) A, An
   - (d) The, A

2. _____ beggar who met us offered us _____ fruit.
   - (a) An, A
   - (b) A, The
   - (c) A, An
   - (d) The, A

3. Sanil's pet was _____ eagle. _____ eagle was friendly.
   - (a) An, The
   - (b) A, The
   - (c) A, An
   - (d) The, A

4. Sakshi had to wear ____ uniform to school. The uniform had _____ unpleasant smell.
   - (a) An, A
   - (b) A, The
   - (c) A, An
   - (d) The, A

5. _____ elephant entered our village today. _____ villagers were very scared.
   - (a) An, A
   - (b) An, The
   - (c) A, An
   - (d) The, A

III. Select the type of pronouns that have been underlined from the given options:

1. I didn't hurt the man. The fault is all <u>yours</u>.
   - (a) Personal, Possessive
   - (b) Interrogative, Reflexive
   - (c) Demonstrative, Personal
   - (d) Interrogative, Possessive

2. He is an old friend of <u>mine</u>. <u>These</u> are his children.
   - (a) Possessive, Interrogative
   - (b) Interrogative, Reflexive
   - (c) Demonstrative, Personal
   - (d) Possessive, Demonstrative

3. <u>When</u> will the guests arrive? Will they be able to let <u>themselves</u> in?
   - (a) Possessive, Interrogative
   - (b) Interrogative, Reflexive
   - (c) Demonstrative, Personal
   - (d) Possessive, Demonstrative

4. <u>These</u> are their clothes. <u>Where</u> do you want me to keep them?
   - (a) Possessive, Interrogative
   - (b) Interrogative, Reflexive
   - (c) Demonstrative, Personal
   - (d) Demonstrative, Interrogative

5. Will <u>you</u> do all the work <u>yourself</u>?
   - (a) Possessive, Interrogative
   - (b) Personal, Reflexive
   - (c) Demonstrative, Personal
   - (d) Demonstrative, Interrogative

IV. Pick the option that fits the underlined phrases from the given alternatives:

1. We <u>are answering</u> question number one. We <u>will finish</u> it soon.
   (a) Simple Present Tense, Simple Past Tense
   (b) Future Continuous Tense, Present Continuous Tense
   (c) Present Continuous Tense, Simple Future Tense
   (d) Past Continuous Tense, Simple Future Tense

2. Geeta <u>ate</u> her lunch. She <u>eats</u> at one o'clock every day.
   (a) Simple Past Tense, Simple Present Tense
   (b) Future Continuous Tense, Present Continuous Tense
   (c) Present Continuous Tense, Simple Future Tense
   (d) Past Continuous Tense, Simple Future Tense

3. The boy <u>was playing</u> a board game. He <u>will be going</u> to bed soon.
   (a) Simple Past Tense, Simple Present Tense
   (b) Future Continuous Tense, Present Continuous Tense
   (c) Present Continuous Tense, Simple Future Tense
   (d) Past Continuous Tense, Future Continuous Tense

4. I <u>will wash</u> my hands later. I <u>wash</u> them every evening.
   (a) Simple Past Tense, Simple Present Tense
   (b) Simple Future Tense, Simple Present Tense
   (c) Present Continuous Tense, Simple Future Tense
   (d) Past Continuous Tense, Simple Future Tense

5. Nikita <u>will be jumping</u> for joy soon. Her pet dog <u>recovered</u> from its illness.
   (a) Simple Past Tense, Simple Present Tense
   (b) Future Continuous Tense, Present Continuous Tense
   (c) Present Continuous Tense, Simple Future Tense
   (d) Future Continuous Tense, Simple Past Tense

V. Pick the correct preposition from the options and fill in the blanks:

1. Tarun placed the utensils _____ the sink.
   (a) Over   (b) Under
   (c) Towards   (d) In

2. The car arrived _____ the flight had landed.
   (a) After   (b) During
   (c) Under   (d) With

3. The broom was kept_____ the dustpan.
   (a) In   (b) Beside
   (c) After   (d) Towards

4. The boy kept the pencil _____ the book.
   (a) Towards   (b) From
   (c) Over   (d) Beyond

5. The song of the nightingale came from _____ the fence.
   (a) Beyond   (b) Under
   (c) Before   (d) In

VI. Fill in the blanks with the correct collocation:

1. You could _____ if you stare at the Sun for too long.
   (a) Come fast   (b) Sing aloud
   (c) Go blind   (d) Save time

2. Sneha's surprise birthday party was a _____.
   (a) Full success
   (b) Simple failure
   (c) Slight surprise
   (d) Complete success

3. I think India will become a wonderful country in the _____.
   (a) Near future
   (b) Recent future
   (c) Uncertain future
   (d) Recent past

4. The police arrested the _____ at their hideout.
   (a) Collection of thugs
   (b) Party of thieves
   (c) Club of thieves
   (d) Gang of thieves

5. I am _____ of my bad behavior last night.
   (a) Deeply sorry
   (b) Slightly regretting
   (c) Deeply ashamed
   (d) Terribly sorrowful

VII. Pick the words with the correct spellings and fill in the blanks:

1. I wish that I could _____ a _____ that makes such tasty honey.
   (a) Bee, be   (b) Bee, bee
   (c) Be, be   (d) Be, bee

2. I have _____ of a plan to make me _____.
   (a) Conceived, famous
   (b) Concieved, fameous
   (c) Cuncieved, famos
   (d) Cunceived, famus

3. There are _____ on our table and _____ in our fireplace.
   (a) Knives, cinders   (b) Knifes, sinders
   (c) Nives, synders   (d) Nifes, cinders

4. The man was _____ to live _____.
   (a) Triing, cheeryly
   (b) Traing, cheeriously
   (c) Trying, cheerily
   (d) Triying, cherily

5. The _____ were caught because they _____ over the doorstep.
   (a) Theifs, trippeed   (b) Theives, triped
   (c) Thiefs, triipped   (d) Thieves, tripped

VIII. Match the animal with the sound it makes:

Animal	Sound
1. Geese	(a) Bleat
2. Elephant	(b) Hoot
3. Snake	(c) Cackle
4. Owl	(d) Trumpet
5. Giraffe	(e) Hiss

IX. See the collocation and the correct usage of words and choose the correct option:

Note: T stands for True whereas F stands for False

1. The little boy saw the tiger and was afraid. The tiger saw the little boy and became sad.
   (a) T, T   (b) T, F
   (c) F, T   (d) F, F

2. The sight of dirty socks makes me sad. The sight of dirty socks disgusts me.
   (a) T, T   (b) T, F
   (c) F, T   (d) F, F

3. When Ravi lied to his father, his father got very angry. Ravi was surprised his father found out that he had lied.
   (a) T, T   (b) T, F
   (c) F, T   (d) F, F

4. Sonam was happy when the teacher punished her. The sight of cute puppies disgusted Rita.
   (a) T, T   (b) T, F
   (c) F, T   (d) F, F

5. The sight of snakes terrifies Vimal. He is also easily irritated by bees.
   (a) T, T   (b) T, F
   (c) F, T   (d) F, F

X. Find the option that best describes the part of body given in the question:

1. Thumb:
   (a) A finger on both feet because of which we can run faster.
   (b) The body part attached to the top of the upper arm.
   (c) The part of the thorax that protects the heart.
   (d) A finger on each hand that folds inwards and helps us to pick things up.

2. Eyebrow:
   (a) A band of hair above each eye that stops sweat from entering the eye.
   (b) A hole below the eyes that allows us to breathe through it.
   (c) The cover above our eyes that allows us to close them.
   (d) The hair on the eyelids that stop tiny objects from entering the eyes.

3. Shoulder:
   (a) The part of the torso that helps with the digestion of food.
   (b) The part that joins the upper leg with the lower leg.
   (c) The part of the torso that lies on each side of the neck and is used to hang things from.
   (d) The part of the body that is covered with a cap.

4. Foot:
   (a) The part of the arm that contains the digits.
   (b) The part of the body that one covers with socks.
   (c) The part of the body one covers with shirts.
   (d) The part of the body just above the chin.

5. Elbow:
   (a) The body part between the upper arm and forearm. It allows us to bend our arms.
   (b) The body part that attaches the head to the torso.
   (c) The body part between the thigh and the lower leg. It allows us to bend our legs.
   (d) The body part around which we wear pants.

Model Test Paper – 1

SECTION I: Word and Structure Knowledge

Directions (1 – 4): Choose the word with the correct spelling.

1. (a) Fourtune   (b) Fortune
   (c) Phortune   (d) Forteune

2. (a) Successful   (b) Sucesful
   (c) Succesfull   (d) Succesful

3. (a) Deceve   (b) Desieve
   (c) Decieve   (d) Deceive

4. (a) Grammer   (b) Grammar
   (c) Gramar   (d) Gramer

Directions (5 – 8): Match the word with the correct option and find out the correct alternative.

5. Hand
   (a) Leg   (b) Face
   (c) Arm   (d) Ear

6. Table
   (a) Chair   (b) Flower
   (c) Plate   (d) Tablecloth

7. Lock
   (a) Car   (b) Window
   (c) Door   (d) Key

8. Doctor
   (a) House   (b) School
   (c) Hospital   (d) Playground

Directions (9 – 12): Find the odd word from the options given below.

9. (a) Cow   (b) Goose
   (c) Dog   (d) Bike

10. (a) Fields   (b) Story
    (c) Forests   (d) Woods

11. (a) Daisy   (b) Laptop
    (c) Phone   (d) Computer

12. (a) Mother   (b) Brother
    (c) Teacher   (d) Grandfather

Directions (13 – 20): Select the right word to fill in the blank.

13. Shah Rukh Khan is a ___ Bollywood actor.
    (a) Ugly   (b) Unknown
    (c) New   (d) Famous

14. There are _____ in the forests.
    (a) Tigers   (b) Pens
    (c) Cars   (d) Stairs

15. Geeta won the Art competition. She is so _____.
    (a) Funny   (b) Mean
    (c) Creative   (d) Sad

16. A _____ is when people go for a holiday on a boat.
    (a) Road trip   (b) Cruise
    (c) Tour   (d) Drive

17. The volunteers _____ a bridge.
    (a) Built   (b) Made
    (c) Created   (d) Prepared

18. When Mr. Singh reached home, he _____ his door.
    (a) Entered   (b) Locked
    (c) Rung   (d) Unlocked

19. He _____ the child from drowning.
    (a) Fainted   (b) Stopped
    (c) Helped   (d) Saved

20. The police _____ the thief.
    (a) Left   (b) Caught
    (c) Catched   (d) Helped

SECTION II: Reading

Gandhi Jayanti is celebrated yearly on 2nd October. It is one of the three official declared national holidays of India and is observed in all of its states and union territories. The other two national holidays are Independence Day (15th August) and Republic Day (26th January).

Gandhi Jayanti is marked by prayer services and tributes all over India, especially at Raj Ghat,

Gandhi's memorial in New Delhi where he was cremated. Popular activities include prayer meetings, commemorative ceremonies in different cities by colleges, local government institutions and socio-political institutions. Painting and essay competitions are conducted and best awards are granted for projects in schools and the community on themes of glorifying peace, non-violence and Gandhi's effort in the Indian Freedom Struggle.

On the basis of the above paragraph, complete the sentences.

21. Gandhi Jayanti is celebrated on _____ .
    (a) 12 October
    (b) 2 October
    (c) 2 June
    (d) 4 November

22. How many national holidays are there?
    (a) 4
    (b) 2
    (c) 3
    (d) 1

23. Where is Raj Ghat located?
    (a) New Delhi
    (b) Lucknow
    (c) Kolkata
    (d) Chennai

24. How do schools celebrate?
    (a) With songs
    (b) Athletic meets
    (c) Races
    (d) Paintings and Essay competitions

25. Prayer meetings and commemorative ceremonies are held by
    (a) Colleges, Government bodies and others
    (b) Families
    (c) Hospital
    (d) Schools

26. To glorify means:
    (a) To make beautiful
    (b) Describe or represent as admirable
    (c) To demean
    (d) To praise

Dear Annie,

In today's fast world, it's difficult to find a true friend like you. I sometimes think I am very lucky to get you as one; without you life would have been very boring. I still remember the first day of school when we were young, you called me and gave a seat besides you. It's now almost 15 years and our relationship has grown in past years. I would like to thank you for being there for me through the ups and downs of my life.

Last year when my father fell ill, you were a support to me and my family. I don't know what I would have done without you then. You were more helpful than my relatives. I can never forget how you stayed back in the hospital late at night just to support me and my mother.

I cherish every moment of life we spent together. Though you are away from me, I still feel that you are close to me. How are your studies going? Last time when you wrote you seemed a little worried about the portions. I know you will easily pass your engineering course with flying colours.

When are your next holidays? I am eagerly waiting to meet you and spend some time with you.

I would like to thank you for being my friend and being there for me.

With best wishes,

Tarun.

On the basis of the above paragraph, answer the following questions.

27. Who is Annie to Tarun?
    (a) Boss
    (b) Best Friend
    (c) Cousin
    (d) Sister

28. How long have they known each other?
    (a) 15 years
    (b) 10 years
    (c) 7 years
    (d) 13 ears

29. What happened the last year to Tarun ?
    (a) He got promoted
    (b) He got Married
    (c) He got a dog
    (d) His father fell ill.

30. What is Annie worried about?
    (a) Her sister
    (b) Her job
    (c) Her Engineering exams
    (d) Her plants

31. What does Tarun hope to do when he meets Annie next?
    (a) Thank her for being his friend
    (b) Take her for a movie
    (c) Have lunch together
    (d) Go for a picnic

SECTION III: Spoken and Written Expression

Direction (32 – 35): Choose the best reply to complete each conversation.

32. Peter: What a beautiful lake!

    Sam:

    (a) Not really

    (b) I don't care for lakes

    (c) It's okay

    (d) It really is!

33. Anita: May I speak to Lena?

    Monica:

    (a) No

    (b) Yes, please hold while I get her.

    (c) She doesn't want to

    (d) I can't call her

34. Mark: Hello, I'm Mark.

    Ben:

    (a) Hello, my name is Ben.

    (b) I don't care

    (c) So?

    (d) Hmmm, I'm Ben

35. Rachel: How do you do?

    Tom:

    (a) Not very well

    (b) Okay.

    (c) Good and how are you?

    (d) I don't want to answer

Model Test Paper – 2

SECTION I: Word and Structure Knowledge

Directions (1 – 5): Choose the correct sound of the given word from the options.

1. Bee
   (a) Beezzz   (b) Bizz
   (c) Buzz   (d) Buesss

2. Lion
   (a) Roar   (b) Grrrrr
   (c) Snarl   (d) Growl

3. Duck
   (a) Moo   (b) Cackle
   (c) Honk   (d) Quack

4. Seal
   (a) Barks   (b) Yips
   (c) Chatters   (d) Giggles

5. Whale
   (a) Gurgles   (b) Talks
   (c) Wails   (d) Sings

Directions (6 – 10): Find the odd word.

6. (a) Book   (b) Leaf
   (c) Scale   (d) Eraser

7. (a) Banana   (b) Cheese
   (c) Cherry   (d) Mango

8. (a) Feet   (b) Fingers
   (c) Palm   (d) Hand

9. (a) Happy   (b) Joyful
   (c) Gloomy   (d) Cheerful

10. (a) Uniform   (b) Badge
    (c) Bag   (d) Sandwich

Directions (11–14): Make a proper word from the spellings and find out the correct option.

11. Coltionlec
    (a) Tioncollec
    (b) Collection
    (c) Tioncocell
    (d) Cellcotion

12. Refnceere
    (a) Reference   (b) Encerrefe
    (c) Renceefe   (d) Fererence

13. Mediateim
    (a) Diateemim   (b) Immediate
    (c) Mimetedia   (d) Tedimemia

14. Sionadmis
    (a) Dionamiss   (b) Missadion
    (c) Admission   (d) Amisdsion

Directions (15–20): Select the right word to fit the description.

15. My fingers are _____ after writing the exam.
    (a) Sweating   (b) Swelling
    (c) Itching   (d) Cramping

16. Use a dictionary to look _____ these words.
    (a) Down   (b) See
    (c) Through   (d) Up

17. The hole was big enough to look _____.
    (a) At   (b) Through
    (c) In   (d) Out

18. Police have warned the local residents to be on the look-out for an _____ prisoner.
    (a) Escaped   (b) Scary
    (c) Happy   (d) Loose

19. Keith was sitting all ____ himself.
    (a) From   (b) Next to
    (c) By   (d) Apart

20. There was a _____ bang.
    (a) Clear   (b) Noisy
    (c) Loud   (d) Sad

SECTION II: Reading

Sports days, sometimes referred to as field days, are events staged by many schools and offices in which people take part in competitive sporting activities, often with the aim of winning trophies or prizes. Though they are often held at the beginning of summer, they are also staged in the autumn or spring seasons, especially in countries where the summer is very harsh. Schools stage many sports days in which children participate in the sporting events. It is usually held in elementary schools, or grades Kindergarten-8th Grade.

In schools which use a house system, a feature of the school is the competition between the houses; this is especially brought out during sporting events such as an inter-house sports day.

Games that are played on school sports days can be wide and varied. They can include straightforward sprints and longer races for all age groups as well as egg and spoon races. Three legged races are run as well as sack races and parent and child races.

On the basis of the above paragraph, answer these questions.

21. What are field days known as?
    (a) Sports day
    (b) Match Day
    (c) House Day
    (d) Race Day

22. What does 'Competitive' mean?
    (a) Relating to computers
    (b) Relating to competition
    (c) To be spirited
    (d) To compute

23. What do the participants win after participating ?
    (a) Hugs
    (b) Cars
    (c) Money
    (d) Trophies or Prizes

24. Explain Inter-house Sports day.
    (a) Children from the same housing complex compete against others
    (b) Children run from one house to another
    (c) Schools who feature the house system make it an event for competition between the houses
    (d) Houses play sports

25. Do offices also have sports days?
    (a) I don't know   (b) Yes
    (c) No   (d) May be

26. Is Sports day only for children?
    (a) No
    (b) Yes
    (c) No, offices as well as parents participate in some races
    (d) None of these

27. Which of these sports take place on Sports day?
    (a) Hurdles
    (b) Long jump
    (c) Hopping races
    (d) Long sprints and three legged races

SECTION III: Spoken and Written Expression

Directions (28 – 32): Choose the best reply to complete each conversation.

28. Zara: I think my laptop needs to be repaired.
    Nicki:
    (a) I'll give you the number of the repair shop I use.
    (b) I can't help you.
    (c) So fix it.
    (d) None of these.

29. Tim: Hi, my name is Tim.
    Peter:
    (a) Hello
    (b) Okay
    (c) Hey, my name is Peter.
    (d) None of these.

30. Nina: Do you need some help with the poster?
    Teena:
    (a) Yes, thank you for offering.
    (b) I don't need your help.
    (c) No, thanks.
    (d) None of these.

31. Sourav: Oh no! I lost my pen.
    Indu:
    (a) Sorry, I can't help you.
    (b) I'll help you search for it.
    (c) It doesn't concern me.
    (d) None of these.

2. Sara: How long is the flight to Mumbai?
   Moni:
   (a) It doesn't matter to me.
   (b) Please don't ask me.
   (c) Two and a half hours, if my estimation is
       correct.
   (d) None of these.

Direction (33 – 35): Choose the best option to complete the passage.

3. Leela and Maya love to play 'Kitchen'.
   They spent the whole day pretending to cook
   fancy dishes. When they grow up they want
   to_____.
   (a) Live in a kitchen
   (b) Become engineers
   (c) Become chefs

   (d) None of these

34. Meena loves her grandfather very much.
    His favourite activity is to paint. So, Meena
    gave some _____ to her grandfather for his
    birthday.
    (a) Paint equipment
    (b) A painting
    (c) A brush
    (d) None of these.

35. Ravi gets the highest marks in class. He
    _____ and is dedicated to his studies.
    (a) Doesn't study
    (b) Works hard
    (c) Studies.
    (d) None of these.

Hints and Solutions

SECTION 1: WORD AND STRUCTURE KNOWLEDGE

1. SPELLINGS

Answer Key

I

1. (b)	2. (a)	3. (d)	4. (d)	5. (c)	6. (a)	7. (c)	8. (b)	9. (c)	10. (a)
11. (c)	12. (a)	13. (d)	14. (a)	15. (c)	16. (b)	17. (c)	18. (d)		

II

1. (b)	2. (c)	3. (a)	4. (c)	5. (d)	6. (a)

III

1. (b)	2. (a)	3. (c)	4. (b)	5. (d)	6. (d)

2. COLLOCATIONS

Answer Key

I

1. (b)	2. (c)	3. (b)	4. (d)	5. (a)	6. (c)	7. (a)	8. (b)	9. (b)	10. (c)
11. (d)	12. (b)	13. (d)	14. (a)	15. (d)	16. (b)	17. (c)	18. (d)	19. (c)	20. (d)

II

1. (a)	2. (d)	3. (a)	4. (d)	5. (a)	6. (d)	7. (c)	8. (c)	9. (c)	10. (b)

3. ANIMALS AND THEIR SOUNDS, FOOD HABITS AND HOMES

	Answer Key								
				I.					
1. (c)	2. (b)	3. (d)	4. (a)	5. (c)	6. (d)	7. (c)	8. (a)	9. (c)	10. (d)
				II.					
1. (g)	2. (c)	3. (f)	4. (h)	5. (i)	6. (i)	7. (b)	8. (d)	9. (a)	10. (e)
				III					
1. (a)	2. (c)	3. (b)	4. (b)	5. (c)	6. (a)	7. (c)	8. (a)	9. (c)	10. (a)

4. PARTS OF BODY AND CLOTHES

	Answer Key								
				I.					
1. (b)	2. (b)	3. (c)	4. (a)	5. (c)	6. (d)	7. (d)	8. (c)	9. (b)	10. (b)
				II.					
1. (f)	2. (i)	3. (h)	4. (j)	5. (c)	6. (b)	7. (d)	8. (e)	9. (g)	10. (a)
				III.					
1. (c)	2. (b)	3. (d)	4. (c)	5. (a)	6. (d)	7. (a)	8. (c)	9. (b)	10. (c)

5. BASIC EMOTIONS

	Answer Key								
				I.					
1. (c)	2. (b)	3. (c)	4. (a)	5. (d)	6. (d)	7. (b)	8. (c)	9. (b)	10. (a)
				II.					
1. (b)	2. (b)	3. (d)	4. (c)	5. (a)	6. (d)	7. (d)	8. (a)	9. (b)	10. (c)
				III.					
1. (b)	2. (c)	3. (d)	4. (c)	5. (a)	6. (a)	7. (a)	8. (d)	9. (a)	10. (b)

6. NOUNS

Answer Key

I.

1. (d)	2. (b)	3. (a)	4. (d)	5. (c)	6. (d)				

II.

1. (a)	2. (c)	3. (b)	4. (a)	5. (a)	6. (b)	7. (b)	8. (b)	9. (c)	10. (b)
11. (b)	12. (a)								

III.

1. (b)	2. (a)	3. (c)	4. (d)	5. (b)	6. (b)	7. (c)	8. (a)	9. (a)	10. (a)
11. (a)	12. (b)								

7. PRONOUNS

Answer Key

I.

1. (c)	2. (a)	3. (b)	4. (a)	5. (b)	6. (c)	7. (b)	8. (d)	9. (a)	10. (b)
11. (c)	12. (a)	13. (b)	14. (b)	15. (d)					

II.

1. (c)	2. (b)	3. (a)	4. (d)	5. (b)

III.

1. (d)	2. (a)	3. (c)	4. (b)	5. (a)

IV.

1. (a)	2. (d)	3. (c)	4. (a)	5. (d)

8. VERBS

Answer Key

I.

1. Wear	2. Flew	3. Write	4. Spent	5. Send	6. Left	7. Buy	8. Got	9. Told	10. Come
11. Hit	12. Drank	13. Ran	14. Read	15. Was					

II.

1. (d)	2. (c)	3. (a)	4. (c)	5. (d)	6. (b)	7. (c)	8. (d)	9. (b)	10. (a)
11. (c)	12. (d)	13. (c)	14. (b)	15. (c)					

9. ADVERBS

Answer Key

I.

1. (b)	2. (c)	3. (d)	4. (c)	5. (d)	6. (b)	7. (a)	8. (c)	9. (b)	10. (d)
11. (a)	12. (c)	13. (b)	14. (c)	15. (a)	16. (d)	17. (b)	18. (c)	19. (a)	20. (c)

II.

1. Tomorrow	2. Always	3. Really	4. Obediently	5. Happily
6. Sometimes	7. On	8. Already	9. Twice	10. Lazily

10. ADJECTIVE

Answer Key

I.

1. (a)	2. (d)	3. (c)	4. (a)	5. (b)	6. (a)	7. (d)	8. (c)	9. (a)	

II.

1. (a)	2. (a)	3. (c)	4. (d)	5. (b)	6. (a)	7. (a)	8. (d)	9. (a)	10. (d)

11. ARTICLES

Answer Key

I.

1. (c)	2. (d)	3. (b)	4. (d)	5. (c)	6. (a)	7. (d)	8. (c)	9. (b)	10. (c)
11. (d)	12. (b)	13. (b)	14. (c)	15. (a)					

II.

1. (b)	2. (c)	3. (b)	4. (b)	5. (c)	6. (b)	7. (a)	8. (a)	9. (c)	10. (d)
11. (b)	12. (a)	13. (c)	14. (a)	15. (c)					

12. PREPOSITIONS

Answer Key

I.

1. (b)	2. (c)	3. (a)	4. (d)	5. (c)	6. (c)	7. (d)	8. (a)	9. (d)	10. (b)
11. (d)	12. (a)	13. (c)	14. (a)	15. (d)	16. (a)	17. (c)	18. (d)	19. (c)	20. (c)
21. (b)	22. (c)	23. (d)	24. (d)	25. (b)	26. (c)	27. (a)	28. (b)	29. (c)	30. (a)
31. (b)	32. (b)	33. (a)	34. (b)	35. (d)					

II.

1. in	2. in	3. by	4. ago	5. in	6. by	7. till	8. thorough	9. in	10. at

III.

1. (a)	2. (c)	3. (a)	4. (a)	5. (a)	6. (c)	7. (a)	8. (a)	9. (c)	10. (c)
11. (a)	12. (a)	13. (a)	14. (a)	15. (a)					

13. CONJUNCTIONS

Answer Key									
1. (a)	2. (b)	3. (a)	4. (b)	5. (a)	6. (c)	7. (c)	8. (c)	9. (d)	10. (a)
11. (b)	12. (b)	13. (a)	14. (c)	15. (b)	16. (b)	17. (b)	18. (c)	19. (c)	20. (c)

14. SIMPLE TENSES

Answer Key				
I				
1. Go	2. Not rain	3. Saw	4. Eat	5. Will see
6. Is	7. Left	8. Will go	9. Play	10. Ate
11. Drove	12. Drink	13. Came	14. Did not like	15. Will be late

II									
1. (c)	2. (a)	3. (c)	4. (d)	5. (b)	6. (c)	7. (d)	8. (b)	9. (d)	10. (a)
11. (b)	12. (c)	13. (d)	14. (b)	15. (a)					

15. PUNCTUATION

Answer Key									
1. (c)	2. (b)	3. (d)	4. (c)	5. (d)	6. (a)	7. (b)	8. (c)	9. (d)	10. (a)
11. (a)	12. (c)	13. (a)	14. (b)	15. (a)	16. (a)	17. (a)	18. (a)	19. (b)	

SECTION 2: READING COMPREHENSION

TIPS ON READING COMPREHENSION

Answer Key

Comprehension 1

1. Milo is a lion cub.

2. The name of Milo's zebra friend is Abu.

3. Mr. Khalif takes Milo to camp in the dense forest because he wants to raise a brave lion.

4. Abu is very good at playing ludo.

5. Mrs. Khalif bakes delicious cakes for Abu and Milo.

6. Abu often tells Mr. Khalif that he is a very good king of the jungle and that all animals love him.

Comprehension 2

1. The story is about Derbie, a car.

2. Derbie was the fastest car in town.

3. Mr. Biswas is the owner of Derbie.

4. The mechanic at the garage would give Derbie a good wash and change its tyres, if there was a need.

5. Derbie is very special to Mr. Biswas as it is his first car. It is the car in which Mr. Biswas had brought his newly born son to his home.

6. Mr. Biswas takes Derbie to the town every Sunday.

Comprehension 3

1. Mrs. Sen is the drama teacher of Kshitij and Zaira.

2. Mrs. Sen gives Kshitij and Zaira the responsibility of selecting a play for the school morning assembly.

3. Zaira's mother writes plays. She is a playwright.

4. Mrs. Sen wants Kshitij and Zaira to choose a comedy because she wants everybody to have a good start to their day.

5. Kshitij suggests that they should play a scene from the Harry Potter movie.
6. Mrs. Sen wants to discuss the idea with the drama club.
Comprehension 4
1. Ashima and Bharat are sister and brother.
2. Bharat called home to say that he needs their father to pick him up from the station.
3. Bharat is coming by the Rajdhani Express at 7.00 p.m.
4. Ashima is going for her Maths tuition class.
5. Ashima will be back by 7.30 p.m.
6. Mr Kapoor's car keys are in the bottom drawer of his study desk.
Comprehension 5
1. The occasion of the invitation is a marriage ceremony.
2. Federick Pablo and Sunita Pinto are getting married to each other.
3. Mrs. and Mr. Pablo's son is getting married.
4. Mrs. and Mr. Pinto's daughter is getting married.
5. The marriage is taking place on Saturday, 22nd June 2019.
6. The venue of the marriage is Sacred Heart Church, Mapusa, Goa.

Hints and Solutions

SECTION 3: SPOKEN AND WRITTEN EXPRESSIONS

LET'S SPEAK

Answer Key

I.

1. (c)	2. (b)	3. (d)	4. (d)	5. (b)	6. (a)	7. (b)	8. (d)	9. (b)	10. (d)
11. (c)	12. (c)	13. (a)	14. (b)	15. (b)					

II.

1. (a) I am fine;	(b) Nice to meet you;	(c) Congratulations;	(d) Thank you;	(e) See you later
2. (a) Rahul;	(b) Pleased to meet you;	(c) Please;	(d) Thank you;	(e) Sure
3. (a) May;	(b) I am afraid;	(c) Is it;	(d) Yes;	(e) Thank you

SECTION 4: ACHIEVERS' SECTION

HIGHER ORDER THINKING SKILLS (HOTS)

	Answer Key				
I.	1. (b)	2. (a)	3. (c)	4. (d)	5. (b)
II.	1. (c)	2. (d)	3. (a)	4. (c)	5. (b)
III.	1. (a)	2. (d)	3. (b)	4. (d)	5. (b)
IV.	1. (c)	2. (a)	3. (d)	4. (b)	5. (d)
V.	1. (d)	2. (a)	3. (b)	4. (c)	5. (a)
VI.	1. (c)	2. (d)	3. (a)	4. (d)	5. (c)
VII.	1. (d)	2. (a)	3. (a)	4. (c)	5. (d)
VIII.	1. (c)	2. (d)	3. (e)	4. (b)	5. (a)
IX.	1. (b)	2. (c)	3. (a)	4. (d)	5. (a)
X.	1. (d)	2. (a)	3. (c)	4. (b)	5. (a)

MODEL TEST PAPER – 1

Answer Key

I.

1. (b)	2. (a)	3. (d)	4. (b)	5. (c)	6. (a)	7. (d)	8. (c)	9. (d)	10. (b)
11. (a)	12. (c)	13. (d)	14. (a)	15. (c)	16. (b)	17. (a)	18. (d)	19. (d)	20. (b)

II.

21. (b)	22. (c)	23. (a)	24. (d)	25. (a)	26. (b)	27. (b)	28. (a)	29. (d)	30. (c)
31. (a)									

III.

32. (d)	33. (b)	34. (a)	35. (c)						

MODEL TEST PAPER – 2

Answer Key

I.

1. (c)	2. (a)	3. (d)	4. (a)	5. (d)	6. (b)	7. (b)	8. (a)	9. (c)	10. (d)
11. (b)	12. (a)	13. (b)	14. (c)	15. (b)	16. (d)	17. (b)	18. (a)	19. (c)	20. (c)

II.

21. (a)	22. (b)	23. (d)	24. (c)	25. (b)	26. (a)	27. (d)			

III.

28. (a)	29. (c)	30. (a)	31. (b)	32. (c)	33. (c)	34. (a)	35. (b)		

OMR ANSWER SHEET

1. NAME (IN ENGLISH CAPITAL LETTERS ONLY)

2. FATHER'S NAME (IN ENGLISH CAPITAL LETTERS ONLY)

Students must write and darken the respective circles completely for School Code, Class and Roll No. columns, othewise their Answer Sheets will not be evaluated.

3. SCHOOL CODE

Columns with letter circles (A–Z) and number circles (0–9).

4. % of Marks / Grade
In Last Class

Percentage OR Grade

Number circles (0–9) for Percentage columns; Grade circles (A–J).

5. CLASS

Number circles (0, 1, 2) and (0–9, M, B)

6. ROLL NO.

Number circles (0–9)

7. GENDER

MALE ○
FEMALE ○

8. STREAM
(Only for Class XI and XII Students)

MATHEMATICS ○
BIOLOGY ○
OTHERS ○

9. MARK YOUR ANSWERS WITH HB PENCIL/BALL POINT PEN (BLUE/BLACK)

No.					No.				
1.	Ⓐ	Ⓑ	Ⓒ	Ⓓ	26.	Ⓐ	Ⓑ	Ⓒ	Ⓓ
2.	Ⓐ	Ⓑ	Ⓒ	Ⓓ	27.	Ⓐ	Ⓑ	Ⓒ	Ⓓ
3.	Ⓐ	Ⓑ	Ⓒ	Ⓓ	28.	Ⓐ	Ⓑ	Ⓒ	Ⓓ
4.	Ⓐ	Ⓑ	Ⓒ	Ⓓ	29.	Ⓐ	Ⓑ	Ⓒ	Ⓓ
5.	Ⓐ	Ⓑ	Ⓒ	Ⓓ	30.	Ⓐ	Ⓑ	Ⓒ	Ⓓ
6.	Ⓐ	Ⓑ	Ⓒ	Ⓓ	31.	Ⓐ	Ⓑ	Ⓒ	Ⓓ
7.	Ⓐ	Ⓑ	Ⓒ	Ⓓ	32.	Ⓐ	Ⓑ	Ⓒ	Ⓓ
8.	Ⓐ	Ⓑ	Ⓒ	Ⓓ	33.	Ⓐ	Ⓑ	Ⓒ	Ⓓ
9.	Ⓐ	Ⓑ	Ⓒ	Ⓓ	34.	Ⓐ	Ⓑ	Ⓒ	Ⓓ
10.	Ⓐ	Ⓑ	Ⓒ	Ⓓ	35.	Ⓐ	Ⓑ	Ⓒ	Ⓓ
11.	Ⓐ	Ⓑ	Ⓒ	Ⓓ	36.	Ⓐ	Ⓑ	Ⓒ	Ⓓ
12.	Ⓐ	Ⓑ	Ⓒ	Ⓓ	37.	Ⓐ	Ⓑ	Ⓒ	Ⓓ
13.	Ⓐ	Ⓑ	Ⓒ	Ⓓ	38.	Ⓐ	Ⓑ	Ⓒ	Ⓓ
14.	Ⓐ	Ⓑ	Ⓒ	Ⓓ	39.	Ⓐ	Ⓑ	Ⓒ	Ⓓ
15.	Ⓐ	Ⓑ	Ⓒ	Ⓓ	40.	Ⓐ	Ⓑ	Ⓒ	Ⓓ
16.	Ⓐ	Ⓑ	Ⓒ	Ⓓ	41.	Ⓐ	Ⓑ	Ⓒ	Ⓓ
17.	Ⓐ	Ⓑ	Ⓒ	Ⓓ	42.	Ⓐ	Ⓑ	Ⓒ	Ⓓ
18.	Ⓐ	Ⓑ	Ⓒ	Ⓓ	43.	Ⓐ	Ⓑ	Ⓒ	Ⓓ
19.	Ⓐ	Ⓑ	Ⓒ	Ⓓ	44.	Ⓐ	Ⓑ	Ⓒ	Ⓓ
20.	Ⓐ	Ⓑ	Ⓒ	Ⓓ	45.	Ⓐ	Ⓑ	Ⓒ	Ⓓ
21.	Ⓐ	Ⓑ	Ⓒ	Ⓓ	46.	Ⓐ	Ⓑ	Ⓒ	Ⓓ
22.	Ⓐ	Ⓑ	Ⓒ	Ⓓ	47.	Ⓐ	Ⓑ	Ⓒ	Ⓓ
23.	Ⓐ	Ⓑ	Ⓒ	Ⓓ	48.	Ⓐ	Ⓑ	Ⓒ	Ⓓ
24.	Ⓐ	Ⓑ	Ⓒ	Ⓓ	49.	Ⓐ	Ⓑ	Ⓒ	Ⓓ
25.	Ⓐ	Ⓑ	Ⓒ	Ⓓ	50.	Ⓐ	Ⓑ	Ⓒ	Ⓓ

V&S Publisher, Head Office: F-2/16 Ansari Road, Daryaganj, New Delhi-110002, Ph: 011-23240026-27, Email:info@vspublishers.com
Regional Office: 5-1-707/1, Brij Bhawan (Beside Central Bank of India Lane) Bank Street, Koti, Hyderabad-500 095,
Ph: 040-24737290, Email: vspublishershyd@gmail.com

OMR ANSWER SHEET

1. NAME (IN ENGLISH CAPITAL LETTERS ONLY)

2. FATHER'S NAME (IN ENGLISH CAPITAL LETTERS ONLY)

Students must write and darken the respective circles completely for School Code, Class and Roll No. columns, othewise their Answer Sheets will not be evaluated.

3. SCHOOL CODE

A B C D E F G H I J K L M N O P Q R S T U V W X Y Z
0 1 2 3 4 5 6 7 8 9

4. % of Marks | Grade

In Last Class

Percentage	OR	Grade

0 1 2 3 4 5 6 7 8 9

A B C D E F G H I J

5. CLASS

0 1 2 4 5 6 7 8 9 M B

6. ROLL NO.

0 1 2 3 4 5 6 7 8 9

7. GENDER

MALE ○
FEMALE ○

8. STREAM
(Only for Class XI and XII Students)

MATHEMATICS ○
BIOLOGY ○
OTHERS ○

9. MARK YOUR ANSWERS WITH HB PENCIL/BALL POINT PEN (BLUE/BLACK)

#					#				
1.	Ⓐ	Ⓑ	Ⓒ	Ⓓ	26.	Ⓐ	Ⓑ	Ⓒ	Ⓓ
2.	Ⓐ	Ⓑ	Ⓒ	Ⓓ	27.	Ⓐ	Ⓑ	Ⓒ	Ⓓ
3.	Ⓐ	Ⓑ	Ⓒ	Ⓓ	28.	Ⓐ	Ⓑ	Ⓒ	Ⓓ
4.	Ⓐ	Ⓑ	Ⓒ	Ⓓ	29.	Ⓐ	Ⓑ	Ⓒ	Ⓓ
5.	Ⓐ	Ⓑ	Ⓒ	Ⓓ	30.	Ⓐ	Ⓑ	Ⓒ	Ⓓ
6.	Ⓐ	Ⓑ	Ⓒ	Ⓓ	31.	Ⓐ	Ⓑ	Ⓒ	Ⓓ
7.	Ⓐ	Ⓑ	Ⓒ	Ⓓ	32.	Ⓐ	Ⓑ	Ⓒ	Ⓓ
8.	Ⓐ	Ⓑ	Ⓒ	Ⓓ	33.	Ⓐ	Ⓑ	Ⓒ	Ⓓ
9.	Ⓐ	Ⓑ	Ⓒ	Ⓓ	34.	Ⓐ	Ⓑ	Ⓒ	Ⓓ
10.	Ⓐ	Ⓑ	Ⓒ	Ⓓ	35.	Ⓐ	Ⓑ	Ⓒ	Ⓓ
11.	Ⓐ	Ⓑ	Ⓒ	Ⓓ	36.	Ⓐ	Ⓑ	Ⓒ	Ⓓ
12.	Ⓐ	Ⓑ	Ⓒ	Ⓓ	37.	Ⓐ	Ⓑ	Ⓒ	Ⓓ
13.	Ⓐ	Ⓑ	Ⓒ	Ⓓ	38.	Ⓐ	Ⓑ	Ⓒ	Ⓓ
14.	Ⓐ	Ⓑ	Ⓒ	Ⓓ	39.	Ⓐ	Ⓑ	Ⓒ	Ⓓ
15.	Ⓐ	Ⓑ	Ⓒ	Ⓓ	40.	Ⓐ	Ⓑ	Ⓒ	Ⓓ
16.	Ⓐ	Ⓑ	Ⓒ	Ⓓ	41.	Ⓐ	Ⓑ	Ⓒ	Ⓓ
17.	Ⓐ	Ⓑ	Ⓒ	Ⓓ	42.	Ⓐ	Ⓑ	Ⓒ	Ⓓ
18.	Ⓐ	Ⓑ	Ⓒ	Ⓓ	43.	Ⓐ	Ⓑ	Ⓒ	Ⓓ
19.	Ⓐ	Ⓑ	Ⓒ	Ⓓ	44.	Ⓐ	Ⓑ	Ⓒ	Ⓓ
20.	Ⓐ	Ⓑ	Ⓒ	Ⓓ	45.	Ⓐ	Ⓑ	Ⓒ	Ⓓ
21.	Ⓐ	Ⓑ	Ⓒ	Ⓓ	46.	Ⓐ	Ⓑ	Ⓒ	Ⓓ
22.	Ⓐ	Ⓑ	Ⓒ	Ⓓ	47.	Ⓐ	Ⓑ	Ⓒ	Ⓓ
23.	Ⓐ	Ⓑ	Ⓒ	Ⓓ	48.	Ⓐ	Ⓑ	Ⓒ	Ⓓ
24.	Ⓐ	Ⓑ	Ⓒ	Ⓓ	49.	Ⓐ	Ⓑ	Ⓒ	Ⓓ
25.	Ⓐ	Ⓑ	Ⓒ	Ⓓ	50.	Ⓐ	Ⓑ	Ⓒ	Ⓓ

V&S Publisher, Head Office: F-2/16 Ansari Road, Daryaganj, New Delhi-110002, Ph: 011-23240026-27, Email:info@vspublishers.com
Regional Office: 5-1-707/1, Brij Bhawan (Beside Central Bank of India Lane) Bank Street, Koti, Hyderabad-500 095,
Ph: 040-24737290, Email: vspublishershyd@gmail.com

OMR ANSWER SHEET

1. NAME (IN ENGLISH CAPITAL LETTERS ONLY)

2. FATHER'S NAME (IN ENGLISH CAPITAL LETTERS ONLY)

Students must write and darken the respective circles completely for School Code, Class and Roll No. columns, othewise their Answer Sheets will not be evaluated.

3. SCHOOL CODE

A B C D E F G H I J K L M N O P Q R S T U V W X Y Z

0 1 2 3 4 5 6 7 8 9

4. % of Marks | Grade

In Last Class

| Percentage | OR | Grade |

0 1 2 3 4 5 6 7 8 9

A B C D E F G H I J

5. CLASS

0 1 2

6. ROLL NO.

0 1 2 3 4 5 6 7 8 9

7. GENDER

MALE ○
FEMALE ○

8. STREAM
(Only for Class XI and XII Students)

MATHEMATICS ○
BIOLOGY ○
OTHERS ○

9. MARK YOUR ANSWERS WITH HB PENCIL/BALL POINT PEN (BLUE/BLACK)

1.	A B C D	26.	A B C D
2.	A B C D	27.	A B C D
3.	A B C D	28.	A B C D
4.	A B C D	29.	A B C D
5.	A B C D	30.	A B C D
6.	A B C D	31.	A B C D
7.	A B C D	32.	A B C D
8.	A B C D	33.	A B C D
9.	A B C D	34.	A B C D
10.	A B C D	35.	A B C D
11.	A B C D	36.	A B C D
12.	A B C D	37.	A B C D
13.	A B C D	38.	A B C D
14.	A B C D	39.	A B C D
15.	A B C D	40.	A B C D
16.	A B C D	41.	A B C D
17.	A B C D	42.	A B C D
18.	A B C D	43.	A B C D
19.	A B C D	44.	A B C D
20.	A B C D	45.	A B C D
21.	A B C D	46.	A B C D
22.	A B C D	47.	A B C D
23.	A B C D	48.	A B C D
24.	A B C D	49.	A B C D
25.	A B C D	50.	A B C D

V&S Publisher, Head Office: F-2/16 Ansari Road, Daryaganj, New Delhi-110002, Ph: 011-23240026-27, Email:info@vspublishers.com
Regional Office: 5-1-707/1, Brij Bhawan (Beside Central Bank of India Lane) Bank Street, Koti, Hyderabad-500 095,
Ph: 040-24737290, Email: vspublishershyd@gmail.com

OMR ANSWER SHEET

1. NAME (IN ENGLISH CAPITAL LETTERS ONLY)

2. FATHER'S NAME (IN ENGLISH CAPITAL LETTERS ONLY)

Students must write and darken the respective circles completely for School Code, Class and Roll No. columns, othewise their Answer Sheets will not be evaluated.

3. SCHOOL CODE

A B C D E F G H I J K L M N O P Q R S T U V W X Y Z

0 1 2 3 4 5 6 7 8 9

4. % of Marks | Grade

In Last Class

Percentage OR Grade

0 1 2 3 4 5 6 7 8 9

A B C D E F G H I J

5. CLASS

0 1 2

0 1 2 3 4 5 6 7 8 9 M B

6. ROLL NO.

0 1 2 3 4 5 6 7 8 9

7. GENDER

MALE ○
FEMALE ○

8. STREAM
(Only for Class XI and XII Students)

MATHEMATICS ○
BIOLOGY ○
OTHERS ○

9. MARK YOUR ANSWERS WITH HB PENCIL/BALL POINT PEN (BLUE/BLACK)

1.	Ⓐ Ⓑ Ⓒ Ⓓ	26.	Ⓐ Ⓑ Ⓒ Ⓓ
2.	Ⓐ Ⓑ Ⓒ Ⓓ	27.	Ⓐ Ⓑ Ⓒ Ⓓ
3.	Ⓐ Ⓑ Ⓒ Ⓓ	28.	Ⓐ Ⓑ Ⓒ Ⓓ
4.	Ⓐ Ⓑ Ⓒ Ⓓ	29.	Ⓐ Ⓑ Ⓒ Ⓓ
5.	Ⓐ Ⓑ Ⓒ Ⓓ	30.	Ⓐ Ⓑ Ⓒ Ⓓ
6.	Ⓐ Ⓑ Ⓒ Ⓓ	31.	Ⓐ Ⓑ Ⓒ Ⓓ
7.	Ⓐ Ⓑ Ⓒ Ⓓ	32.	Ⓐ Ⓑ Ⓒ Ⓓ
8.	Ⓐ Ⓑ Ⓒ Ⓓ	33.	Ⓐ Ⓑ Ⓒ Ⓓ
9.	Ⓐ Ⓑ Ⓒ Ⓓ	34.	Ⓐ Ⓑ Ⓒ Ⓓ
10.	Ⓐ Ⓑ Ⓒ Ⓓ	35.	Ⓐ Ⓑ Ⓒ Ⓓ
11.	Ⓐ Ⓑ Ⓒ Ⓓ	36.	Ⓐ Ⓑ Ⓒ Ⓓ
12.	Ⓐ Ⓑ Ⓒ Ⓓ	37.	Ⓐ Ⓑ Ⓒ Ⓓ
13.	Ⓐ Ⓑ Ⓒ Ⓓ	38.	Ⓐ Ⓑ Ⓒ Ⓓ
14.	Ⓐ Ⓑ Ⓒ Ⓓ	39.	Ⓐ Ⓑ Ⓒ Ⓓ
15.	Ⓐ Ⓑ Ⓒ Ⓓ	40.	Ⓐ Ⓑ Ⓒ Ⓓ
16.	Ⓐ Ⓑ Ⓒ Ⓓ	41.	Ⓐ Ⓑ Ⓒ Ⓓ
17.	Ⓐ Ⓑ Ⓒ Ⓓ	42.	Ⓐ Ⓑ Ⓒ Ⓓ
18.	Ⓐ Ⓑ Ⓒ Ⓓ	43.	Ⓐ Ⓑ Ⓒ Ⓓ
19.	Ⓐ Ⓑ Ⓒ Ⓓ	44.	Ⓐ Ⓑ Ⓒ Ⓓ
20.	Ⓐ Ⓑ Ⓒ Ⓓ	45.	Ⓐ Ⓑ Ⓒ Ⓓ
21.	Ⓐ Ⓑ Ⓒ Ⓓ	46.	Ⓐ Ⓑ Ⓒ Ⓓ
22.	Ⓐ Ⓑ Ⓒ Ⓓ	47.	Ⓐ Ⓑ Ⓒ Ⓓ
23.	Ⓐ Ⓑ Ⓒ Ⓓ	48.	Ⓐ Ⓑ Ⓒ Ⓓ
24.	Ⓐ Ⓑ Ⓒ Ⓓ	49.	Ⓐ Ⓑ Ⓒ Ⓓ
25.	Ⓐ Ⓑ Ⓒ Ⓓ	50.	Ⓐ Ⓑ Ⓒ Ⓓ

V&S Publisher, Head Office: F-2/16 Ansari Road, Daryaganj, New Delhi-110002, Ph: 011-23240026-27, Email:info@vspublishers.com
Regional Office: 5-1-707/1, Brij Bhawan (Beside Central Bank of India Lane) Bank Street, Koti, Hyderabad-500 095,
Ph: 040-24737290, Email: vspublishershyd@gmail.com

OMR ANSWER SHEET

1. NAME (IN ENGLISH CAPITAL LETTERS ONLY)

2. FATHER'S NAME (IN ENGLISH CAPITAL LETTERS ONLY)

Students must write and darken the respective circles completely for School Code, Class and Roll No. columns, othewise their Answer Sheets will not be evaluated.

3. SCHOOL CODE

Columns with letters A–Z and digits 0–9.

4. % of Marks / Grade
In Last Class
Percentage OR Grade (0–9 columns, Grade A–J)

9. MARK YOUR ANSWERS WITH HB PENCIL/BALL POINT PEN (BLUE/BLACK)

No.					No.				
1.	Ⓐ	Ⓑ	Ⓒ	Ⓓ	26.	Ⓐ	Ⓑ	Ⓒ	Ⓓ
2.	Ⓐ	Ⓑ	Ⓒ	Ⓓ	27.	Ⓐ	Ⓑ	Ⓒ	Ⓓ
3.	Ⓐ	Ⓑ	Ⓒ	Ⓓ	28.	Ⓐ	Ⓑ	Ⓒ	Ⓓ
4.	Ⓐ	Ⓑ	Ⓒ	Ⓓ	29.	Ⓐ	Ⓑ	Ⓒ	Ⓓ
5.	Ⓐ	Ⓑ	Ⓒ	Ⓓ	30.	Ⓐ	Ⓑ	Ⓒ	Ⓓ
6.	Ⓐ	Ⓑ	Ⓒ	Ⓓ	31.	Ⓐ	Ⓑ	Ⓒ	Ⓓ
7.	Ⓐ	Ⓑ	Ⓒ	Ⓓ	32.	Ⓐ	Ⓑ	Ⓒ	Ⓓ
8.	Ⓐ	Ⓑ	Ⓒ	Ⓓ	33.	Ⓐ	Ⓑ	Ⓒ	Ⓓ
9.	Ⓐ	Ⓑ	Ⓒ	Ⓓ	34.	Ⓐ	Ⓑ	Ⓒ	Ⓓ
10.	Ⓐ	Ⓑ	Ⓒ	Ⓓ	35.	Ⓐ	Ⓑ	Ⓒ	Ⓓ
11.	Ⓐ	Ⓑ	Ⓒ	Ⓓ	36.	Ⓐ	Ⓑ	Ⓒ	Ⓓ
12.	Ⓐ	Ⓑ	Ⓒ	Ⓓ	37.	Ⓐ	Ⓑ	Ⓒ	Ⓓ
13.	Ⓐ	Ⓑ	Ⓒ	Ⓓ	38.	Ⓐ	Ⓑ	Ⓒ	Ⓓ
14.	Ⓐ	Ⓑ	Ⓒ	Ⓓ	39.	Ⓐ	Ⓑ	Ⓒ	Ⓓ
15.	Ⓐ	Ⓑ	Ⓒ	Ⓓ	40.	Ⓐ	Ⓑ	Ⓒ	Ⓓ
16.	Ⓐ	Ⓑ	Ⓒ	Ⓓ	41.	Ⓐ	Ⓑ	Ⓒ	Ⓓ
17.	Ⓐ	Ⓑ	Ⓒ	Ⓓ	42.	Ⓐ	Ⓑ	Ⓒ	Ⓓ
18.	Ⓐ	Ⓑ	Ⓒ	Ⓓ	43.	Ⓐ	Ⓑ	Ⓒ	Ⓓ
19.	Ⓐ	Ⓑ	Ⓒ	Ⓓ	44.	Ⓐ	Ⓑ	Ⓒ	Ⓓ
20.	Ⓐ	Ⓑ	Ⓒ	Ⓓ	45.	Ⓐ	Ⓑ	Ⓒ	Ⓓ
21.	Ⓐ	Ⓑ	Ⓒ	Ⓓ	46.	Ⓐ	Ⓑ	Ⓒ	Ⓓ
22.	Ⓐ	Ⓑ	Ⓒ	Ⓓ	47.	Ⓐ	Ⓑ	Ⓒ	Ⓓ
23.	Ⓐ	Ⓑ	Ⓒ	Ⓓ	48.	Ⓐ	Ⓑ	Ⓒ	Ⓓ
24.	Ⓐ	Ⓑ	Ⓒ	Ⓓ	49.	Ⓐ	Ⓑ	Ⓒ	Ⓓ
25.	Ⓐ	Ⓑ	Ⓒ	Ⓓ	50.	Ⓐ	Ⓑ	Ⓒ	Ⓓ

5. CLASS
Columns with digits 0, 1, 2, 4, 5, 6, 7, 8, 9, M, B

6. ROLL NO.
Columns with digits 0–9

7. GENDER
MALE ◯
FEMALE ◯

8. STREAM
(Only for Class XI and XII Students)
MATHEMATICS ◯
BIOLOGY ◯
OTHERS ◯

V&S Publisher, Head Office: F-2/16 Ansari Road, Daryaganj, New Delhi-110002, Ph: 011-23240026-27, Email:info@vspublishers.com
Regional Office: 5-1-707/1, Brij Bhawan (Beside Central Bank of India Lane) Bank Street, Koti, Hyderabad-500 095,
Ph: 040-24737290, Email: vspublishershyd@gmail.com

OMR ANSWER SHEET

1. NAME (IN ENGLISH CAPITAL LETTERS ONLY)

2. FATHER'S NAME (IN ENGLISH CAPITAL LETTERS ONLY)

Students must write and darken the respective circles completely for School Code, Class and Roll No. columns, otherwise their Answer Sheets will not be evaluated.

3. SCHOOL CODE

Columns: (A–Z), (A–Z), (0–9), (0–9), (0–9), (0–9)

4. % of Marks | Grade

In Last Class

Percentage OR Grade

Percentage digits: (0–9), (0–9), (0–9)

Grade: (A) (B) (C) (D) (E) (F) (G) (H) (I) (J)

5. CLASS

(0) (1) (2) ... (M) (B)

6. ROLL NO.

(0–9) columns

7. GENDER

MALE ○
FEMALE ○

8. STREAM
(Only for Class XI and XII Students)

MATHEMATICS ○
BIOLOGY ○
OTHERS ○

9. MARK YOUR ANSWERS WITH HB PENCIL/BALL POINT PEN (BLUE/BLACK)

No.					No.				
1.	Ⓐ	Ⓑ	Ⓒ	Ⓓ	26.	Ⓐ	Ⓑ	Ⓒ	Ⓓ
2.	Ⓐ	Ⓑ	Ⓒ	Ⓓ	27.	Ⓐ	Ⓑ	Ⓒ	Ⓓ
3.	Ⓐ	Ⓑ	Ⓒ	Ⓓ	28.	Ⓐ	Ⓑ	Ⓒ	Ⓓ
4.	Ⓐ	Ⓑ	Ⓒ	Ⓓ	29.	Ⓐ	Ⓑ	Ⓒ	Ⓓ
5.	Ⓐ	Ⓑ	Ⓒ	Ⓓ	30.	Ⓐ	Ⓑ	Ⓒ	Ⓓ
6.	Ⓐ	Ⓑ	Ⓒ	Ⓓ	31.	Ⓐ	Ⓑ	Ⓒ	Ⓓ
7.	Ⓐ	Ⓑ	Ⓒ	Ⓓ	32.	Ⓐ	Ⓑ	Ⓒ	Ⓓ
8.	Ⓐ	Ⓑ	Ⓒ	Ⓓ	33.	Ⓐ	Ⓑ	Ⓒ	Ⓓ
9.	Ⓐ	Ⓑ	Ⓒ	Ⓓ	34.	Ⓐ	Ⓑ	Ⓒ	Ⓓ
10.	Ⓐ	Ⓑ	Ⓒ	Ⓓ	35.	Ⓐ	Ⓑ	Ⓒ	Ⓓ
11.	Ⓐ	Ⓑ	Ⓒ	Ⓓ	36.	Ⓐ	Ⓑ	Ⓒ	Ⓓ
12.	Ⓐ	Ⓑ	Ⓒ	Ⓓ	37.	Ⓐ	Ⓑ	Ⓒ	Ⓓ
13.	Ⓐ	Ⓑ	Ⓒ	Ⓓ	38.	Ⓐ	Ⓑ	Ⓒ	Ⓓ
14.	Ⓐ	Ⓑ	Ⓒ	Ⓓ	39.	Ⓐ	Ⓑ	Ⓒ	Ⓓ
15.	Ⓐ	Ⓑ	Ⓒ	Ⓓ	40.	Ⓐ	Ⓑ	Ⓒ	Ⓓ
16.	Ⓐ	Ⓑ	Ⓒ	Ⓓ	41.	Ⓐ	Ⓑ	Ⓒ	Ⓓ
17.	Ⓐ	Ⓑ	Ⓒ	Ⓓ	42.	Ⓐ	Ⓑ	Ⓒ	Ⓓ
18.	Ⓐ	Ⓑ	Ⓒ	Ⓓ	43.	Ⓐ	Ⓑ	Ⓒ	Ⓓ
19.	Ⓐ	Ⓑ	Ⓒ	Ⓓ	44.	Ⓐ	Ⓑ	Ⓒ	Ⓓ
20.	Ⓐ	Ⓑ	Ⓒ	Ⓓ	45.	Ⓐ	Ⓑ	Ⓒ	Ⓓ
21.	Ⓐ	Ⓑ	Ⓒ	Ⓓ	46.	Ⓐ	Ⓑ	Ⓒ	Ⓓ
22.	Ⓐ	Ⓑ	Ⓒ	Ⓓ	47.	Ⓐ	Ⓑ	Ⓒ	Ⓓ
23.	Ⓐ	Ⓑ	Ⓒ	Ⓓ	48.	Ⓐ	Ⓑ	Ⓒ	Ⓓ
24.	Ⓐ	Ⓑ	Ⓒ	Ⓓ	49.	Ⓐ	Ⓑ	Ⓒ	Ⓓ
25.	Ⓐ	Ⓑ	Ⓒ	Ⓓ	50.	Ⓐ	Ⓑ	Ⓒ	Ⓓ

V&S Publisher, Head Office: F-2/16 Ansari Road, Daryaganj, New Delhi-110002, Ph: 011-23240026-27, Email:info@vspublishers.com
Regional Office: 5-1-707/1, Brij Bhawan (Beside Central Bank of India Lane) Bank Street, Koti, Hyderabad-500 095,
Ph: 040-24737290, Email: vspublishershyd@gmail.com

OMR ANSWER SHEET

1. NAME (IN ENGLISH CAPITAL LETTERS ONLY)

2. FATHER'S NAME (IN ENGLISH CAPITAL LETTERS ONLY)

Students must write and darken the respective circles completely for School Code, Class and Roll No. columns, othewise their Answer Sheets will not be evaluated.

3. SCHOOL CODE

A	A	0	0	0	0
B	B	1	1	1	1
C	C	2	2	2	2
D	D	3	3	3	3
E	E	4	4	4	4
F	F	5	5	5	5
G	G	6	6	6	6
H	H	7	7	7	7
I	I	8	8	8	8
J	J	9	9	9	9
K	K				
L	L				
M	M				
N	N				
O	O				
P	P				
Q	Q				
R	R				
S	S				
T	T				
U	U				
V	V				
W	W				
X	X				
Y	Y				
Z	Z				

4. % of Marks | **Grade**

In Last Class

Percentage			OR	Grade
0	0	0		A
1	1	1		B
2	2	2		C
3	3	3		D
4	4	4		E
5	5	5		F
6	6	6		G
7	7	7		H
8	8	8		I
9	9	9		J

5. CLASS		6. ROLL NO.		
0	0	0	0	0
1	1	1	1	1
2	2	2	2	2
	4	3	3	3
	5	4	4	4
	6	5	5	5
	7	6	6	6
	8	7	7	7
	9	8	8	8
	M	9	9	9
	B			

7. GENDER

- MALE ◯
- FEMALE ◯

8. STREAM
(Only for Class XI and XII Students)

- MATHEMATICS ◯
- BIOLOGY ◯
- OTHERS ◯

9. MARK YOUR ANSWERS WITH HB PENCIL/BALL POINT PEN (BLUE/BLACK)

1.	A	B	C	D	26.	A	B	C	D
2.	A	B	C	D	27.	A	B	C	D
3.	A	B	C	D	28.	A	B	C	D
4.	A	B	C	D	29.	A	B	C	D
5.	A	B	C	D	30.	A	B	C	D
6.	A	B	C	D	31.	A	B	C	D
7.	A	B	C	D	32.	A	B	C	D
8.	A	B	C	D	33.	A	B	C	D
9.	A	B	C	D	34.	A	B	C	D
10.	A	B	C	D	35.	A	B	C	D
11.	A	B	C	D	36.	A	B	C	D
12.	A	B	C	D	37.	A	B	C	D
13.	A	B	C	D	38.	A	B	C	D
14.	A	B	C	D	39.	A	B	C	D
15.	A	B	C	D	40.	A	B	C	D
16.	A	B	C	D	41.	A	B	C	D
17.	A	B	C	D	42.	A	B	C	D
18.	A	B	C	D	43.	A	B	C	D
19.	A	B	C	D	44.	A	B	C	D
20.	A	B	C	D	45.	A	B	C	D
21.	A	B	C	D	46.	A	B	C	D
22.	A	B	C	D	47.	A	B	C	D
23.	A	B	C	D	48.	A	B	C	D
24.	A	B	C	D	49.	A	B	C	D
25.	A	B	C	D	50.	A	B	C	D

V&S Publisher, Head Office: F-2/16 Ansari Road, Daryaganj, New Delhi-110002, Ph: 011-23240026-27, *Email:info@vspublishers.com*
Regional Office: 5-1-707/1, Brij Bhawan (Beside Central Bank of India Lane) Bank Street, Koti, Hyderabad-500 095,
Ph: 040-24737290, *Email: vspublishershyd@gmail.com*

OMR ANSWER SHEET

1. NAME (IN ENGLISH CAPITAL LETTERS ONLY)

2. FATHER'S NAME (IN ENGLISH CAPITAL LETTERS ONLY)

Students must write and darken the respective circles completely for School Code, Class and Roll No. columns, othewise their Answer Sheets will not be evaluated.

3. SCHOOL CODE

Columns: A–Z letter columns (two), and 0–9 digit columns (four).

4. % of Marks / Grade
In Last Class

Percentage	OR	Grade

Percentage digits: 0 1 2 3 4 5 6 7 8 9 (three columns)
Grade: A B C D E F G H I J

5. CLASS
Digits: 0 1 2 4 5 6 7 8 9 M B (two columns)

6. ROLL NO.
Digits: 0 1 2 3 4 5 6 7 8 9 (three columns)

7. GENDER
MALE ○
FEMALE ○

8. STREAM
(Only for Class XI and XII Students)
MATHEMATICS ○
BIOLOGY ○
OTHERS ○

9. MARK YOUR ANSWERS WITH HB PENCIL/BALL POINT PEN (BLUE/BLACK)

No.					No.				
1.	A	B	C	D	26.	A	B	C	D
2.	A	B	C	D	27.	A	B	C	D
3.	A	B	C	D	28.	A	B	C	D
4.	A	B	C	D	29.	A	B	C	D
5.	A	B	C	D	30.	A	B	C	D
6.	A	B	C	D	31.	A	B	C	D
7.	A	B	C	D	32.	A	B	C	D
8.	A	B	C	D	33.	A	B	C	D
9.	A	B	C	D	34.	A	B	C	D
10.	A	B	C	D	35.	A	B	C	D
11.	A	B	C	D	36.	A	B	C	D
12.	A	B	C	D	37.	A	B	C	D
13.	A	B	C	D	38.	A	B	C	D
14.	A	B	C	D	39.	A	B	C	D
15.	A	B	C	D	40.	A	B	C	D
16.	A	B	C	D	41.	A	B	C	D
17.	A	B	C	D	42.	A	B	C	D
18.	A	B	C	D	43.	A	B	C	D
19.	A	B	C	D	44.	A	B	C	D
20.	A	B	C	D	45.	A	B	C	D
21.	A	B	C	D	46.	A	B	C	D
22.	A	B	C	D	47.	A	B	C	D
23.	A	B	C	D	48.	A	B	C	D
24.	A	B	C	D	49.	A	B	C	D
25.	A	B	C	D	50.	A	B	C	D

V&S Publisher, Head Office: F-2/16 Ansari Road, Daryaganj, New Delhi-110002, Ph: 011-23240026-27, *Email:info@vspublishers.com*
Regional Office: 5-1-707/1, Brij Bhawan (Beside Central Bank of India Lane) Bank Street, Koti, Hyderabad-500 095,
Ph: 040-24737290, *Email: vspublishershyd@gmail.com*

OMR ANSWER SHEET

1. NAME (IN ENGLISH CAPITAL LETTERS ONLY)

2. FATHER'S NAME (IN ENGLISH CAPITAL LETTERS ONLY)

Students must write and darken the respective circles completely for School Code, Class and Roll No. columns, othewise their Answer Sheets will not be evaluated.

3. SCHOOL CODE

(A) (B) (C) (D) (E) (F) (G) (H) (I) (J) (K) (L) (M) (N) (O) (P) (Q) (R) (S) (T) (U) (V) (W) (X) (Y) (Z)

(0) (1) (2) (3) (4) (5) (6) (7) (8) (9)

4. % of Marks — Grade

In Last Class

Percentage OR Grade

(0) (1) (2) (3) (4) (5) (6) (7) (8) (9)

(A) (B) (C) (D) (E) (F) (G) (H) (I) (J)

5. CLASS

(0) (1) (2) (4) (5) (6) (7) (8) (9) (M) (B)

6. ROLL NO.

(0) (1) (2) (3) (4) (5) (6) (7) (8) (9)

7. GENDER

MALE ○
FEMALE ○

8. STREAM
(Only for Class XI and XII Students)

MATHEMATICS ○
BIOLOGY ○
OTHERS ○

9. MARK YOUR ANSWERS WITH HB PENCIL/BALL POINT PEN (BLUE/BLACK)

No.					No.				
1.	A	B	C	D	26.	A	B	C	D
2.	A	B	C	D	27.	A	B	C	D
3.	A	B	C	D	28.	A	B	C	D
4.	A	B	C	D	29.	A	B	C	D
5.	A	B	C	D	30.	A	B	C	D
6.	A	B	C	D	31.	A	B	C	D
7.	A	B	C	D	32.	A	B	C	D
8.	A	B	C	D	33.	A	B	C	D
9.	A	B	C	D	34.	A	B	C	D
10.	A	B	C	D	35.	A	B	C	D
11.	A	B	C	D	36.	A	B	C	D
12.	A	B	C	D	37.	A	B	C	D
13.	A	B	C	D	38.	A	B	C	D
14.	A	B	C	D	39.	A	B	C	D
15.	A	B	C	D	40.	A	B	C	D
16.	A	B	C	D	41.	A	B	C	D
17.	A	B	C	D	42.	A	B	C	D
18.	A	B	C	D	43.	A	B	C	D
19.	A	B	C	D	44.	A	B	C	D
20.	A	B	C	D	45.	A	B	C	D
21.	A	B	C	D	46.	A	B	C	D
22.	A	B	C	D	47.	A	B	C	D
23.	A	B	C	D	48.	A	B	C	D
24.	A	B	C	D	49.	A	B	C	D
25.	A	B	C	D	50.	A	B	C	D

V&S Publisher, Head Office: F-2/16 Ansari Road, Daryaganj, New Delhi-110002, Ph: 011-23240026-27, Email:info@vspublishers.com
Regional Office: 5-1-707/1, Brij Bhawan (Beside Central Bank of India Lane) Bank Street, Koti, Hyderabad-500 095,
Ph: 040-24737290, Email: vspublishershyd@gmail.com

OMR ANSWER SHEET

1. NAME (IN ENGLISH CAPITAL LETTERS ONLY)

2. FATHER'S NAME (IN ENGLISH CAPITAL LETTERS ONLY)

Students must write and darken the respective circles completely for School Code, Class and Roll No. columns, othewise their Answer Sheets will not be evaluated.

3. SCHOOL CODE

Columns: A–Z (two columns) and 0–9 (four columns)

4. % of Marks / Grade

In Last Class

Percentage OR Grade

Percentage digits: 0–9 (three columns)
Grade: A B C D E F G H I J

5. CLASS

0 1 2 4 5 6 7 8 9 M B (two columns)

6. ROLL NO.

0 1 2 3 4 5 6 7 8 9 (three columns)

7. GENDER

MALE ○

FEMALE ○

8. STREAM
(Only for Class XI and XII Students)

MATHEMATICS ○

BIOLOGY ○

OTHERS ○

9. MARK YOUR ANSWERS WITH HB PENCIL/BALL POINT PEN (BLUE/BLACK)

No.					No.				
1.	A	B	C	D	26.	A	B	C	D
2.	A	B	C	D	27.	A	B	C	D
3.	A	B	C	D	28.	A	B	C	D
4.	A	B	C	D	29.	A	B	C	D
5.	A	B	C	D	30.	A	B	C	D
6.	A	B	C	D	31.	A	B	C	D
7.	A	B	C	D	32.	A	B	C	D
8.	A	B	C	D	33.	A	B	C	D
9.	A	B	C	D	34.	A	B	C	D
10.	A	B	C	D	35.	A	B	C	D
11.	A	B	C	D	36.	A	B	C	D
12.	A	B	C	D	37.	A	B	C	D
13.	A	B	C	D	38.	A	B	C	D
14.	A	B	C	D	39.	A	B	C	D
15.	A	B	C	D	40.	A	B	C	D
16.	A	B	C	D	41.	A	B	C	D
17.	A	B	C	D	42.	A	B	C	D
18.	A	B	C	D	43.	A	B	C	D
19.	A	B	C	D	44.	A	B	C	D
20.	A	B	C	D	45.	A	B	C	D
21.	A	B	C	D	46.	A	B	C	D
22.	A	B	C	D	47.	A	B	C	D
23.	A	B	C	D	48.	A	B	C	D
24.	A	B	C	D	49.	A	B	C	D
25.	A	B	C	D	50.	A	B	C	D

V&S Publisher, Head Office: F-2/16 Ansari Road, Daryaganj, New Delhi-110002, Ph: 011-23240026-27, Email:info@vspublishers.com
Regional Office: 5-1-707/1, Brij Bhawan (Beside Central Bank of India Lane) Bank Street, Koti, Hyderabad-500 095,
Ph: 040-24737290, Email: vspublishershyd@gmail.com

OMR ANSWER SHEET

1. NAME (IN ENGLISH CAPITAL LETTERS ONLY)

2. FATHER'S NAME (IN ENGLISH CAPITAL LETTERS ONLY)

Students must write and darken the respective circles completely for School Code, Class and Roll No. columns, othewise their Answer Sheets will not be evaluated.

3. SCHOOL CODE

Letters A–Z columns, digits 0–9 columns

4. % of Marks | Grade

In Last Class

Percentage	OR	Grade

Digits 0–9, Grade A–J

5. CLASS

Digits 0, 1, 2, 4, 5, 6, 7, 8, 9, M, B

6. ROLL NO.

Digits 0–9

7. GENDER

MALE ○
FEMALE ○

8. STREAM
(Only for Class XI and XII Students)

MATHEMATICS ○
BIOLOGY ○
OTHERS ○

9. MARK YOUR ANSWERS WITH HB PENCIL/BALL POINT PEN (BLUE/BLACK)

#		#	
1.	Ⓐ Ⓑ Ⓒ Ⓓ	26.	Ⓐ Ⓑ Ⓒ Ⓓ
2.	Ⓐ Ⓑ Ⓒ Ⓓ	27.	Ⓐ Ⓑ Ⓒ Ⓓ
3.	Ⓐ Ⓑ Ⓒ Ⓓ	28.	Ⓐ Ⓑ Ⓒ Ⓓ
4.	Ⓐ Ⓑ Ⓒ Ⓓ	29.	Ⓐ Ⓑ Ⓒ Ⓓ
5.	Ⓐ Ⓑ Ⓒ Ⓓ	30.	Ⓐ Ⓑ Ⓒ Ⓓ
6.	Ⓐ Ⓑ Ⓒ Ⓓ	31.	Ⓐ Ⓑ Ⓒ Ⓓ
7.	Ⓐ Ⓑ Ⓒ Ⓓ	32.	Ⓐ Ⓑ Ⓒ Ⓓ
8.	Ⓐ Ⓑ Ⓒ Ⓓ	33.	Ⓐ Ⓑ Ⓒ Ⓓ
9.	Ⓐ Ⓑ Ⓒ Ⓓ	34.	Ⓐ Ⓑ Ⓒ Ⓓ
10.	Ⓐ Ⓑ Ⓒ Ⓓ	35.	Ⓐ Ⓑ Ⓒ Ⓓ
11.	Ⓐ Ⓑ Ⓒ Ⓓ	36.	Ⓐ Ⓑ Ⓒ Ⓓ
12.	Ⓐ Ⓑ Ⓒ Ⓓ	37.	Ⓐ Ⓑ Ⓒ Ⓓ
13.	Ⓐ Ⓑ Ⓒ Ⓓ	38.	Ⓐ Ⓑ Ⓒ Ⓓ
14.	Ⓐ Ⓑ Ⓒ Ⓓ	39.	Ⓐ Ⓑ Ⓒ Ⓓ
15.	Ⓐ Ⓑ Ⓒ Ⓓ	40.	Ⓐ Ⓑ Ⓒ Ⓓ
16.	Ⓐ Ⓑ Ⓒ Ⓓ	41.	Ⓐ Ⓑ Ⓒ Ⓓ
17.	Ⓐ Ⓑ Ⓒ Ⓓ	42.	Ⓐ Ⓑ Ⓒ Ⓓ
18.	Ⓐ Ⓑ Ⓒ Ⓓ	43.	Ⓐ Ⓑ Ⓒ Ⓓ
19.	Ⓐ Ⓑ Ⓒ Ⓓ	44.	Ⓐ Ⓑ Ⓒ Ⓓ
20.	Ⓐ Ⓑ Ⓒ Ⓓ	45.	Ⓐ Ⓑ Ⓒ Ⓓ
21.	Ⓐ Ⓑ Ⓒ Ⓓ	46.	Ⓐ Ⓑ Ⓒ Ⓓ
22.	Ⓐ Ⓑ Ⓒ Ⓓ	47.	Ⓐ Ⓑ Ⓒ Ⓓ
23.	Ⓐ Ⓑ Ⓒ Ⓓ	48.	Ⓐ Ⓑ Ⓒ Ⓓ
24.	Ⓐ Ⓑ Ⓒ Ⓓ	49.	Ⓐ Ⓑ Ⓒ Ⓓ
25.	Ⓐ Ⓑ Ⓒ Ⓓ	50.	Ⓐ Ⓑ Ⓒ Ⓓ

V&S Publisher, Head Office: F-2/16 Ansari Road, Daryaganj, New Delhi-110002, Ph: 011-23240026-27, Email:info@vspublishers.com
Regional Office: 5-1-707/1, Brij Bhawan (Beside Central Bank of India Lane) Bank Street, Koti, Hyderabad-500 095,
Ph: 040-24737290, Email: vspublishershyd@gmail.com

OMR ANSWER SHEET

1. NAME (IN ENGLISH CAPITAL LETTERS ONLY)

2. FATHER'S NAME (IN ENGLISH CAPITAL LETTERS ONLY)

Students must write and darken the respective circles completely for School Code, Class and Roll No. columns, othewise their Answer Sheets will not be evaluated.

3. SCHOOL CODE

(A) (B) (C) (D) (E) (F) (G) (H) (I) (J) (K) (L) (M) (N) (O) (P) (Q) (R) (S) (T) (U) (V) (W) (X) (Y) (Z)

0 1 2 3 4 5 6 7 8 9

4. % of Marks | Grade

In Last Class

Percentage	OR	Grade

0 1 2 3 4 5 6 7 8 9

(A) (B) (C) (D) (E) (F) (G) (H) (I) (J)

5. CLASS

0 1 2

0 1 2 4 5 6 7 8 9 (M) (B)

6. ROLL NO.

0 1 2 3 4 5 6 7 8 9

7. GENDER

MALE ○

FEMALE ○

8. STREAM
(Only for Class XI and XII Students)

MATHEMATICS ○
BIOLOGY ○
OTHERS ○

9. MARK YOUR ANSWERS WITH HB PENCIL/BALL POINT PEN (BLUE/BLACK)

No.	A	B	C	D	No.	A	B	C	D
1.	Ⓐ	Ⓑ	Ⓒ	Ⓓ	26.	Ⓐ	Ⓑ	Ⓒ	Ⓓ
2.	Ⓐ	Ⓑ	Ⓒ	Ⓓ	27.	Ⓐ	Ⓑ	Ⓒ	Ⓓ
3.	Ⓐ	Ⓑ	Ⓒ	Ⓓ	28.	Ⓐ	Ⓑ	Ⓒ	Ⓓ
4.	Ⓐ	Ⓑ	Ⓒ	Ⓓ	29.	Ⓐ	Ⓑ	Ⓒ	Ⓓ
5.	Ⓐ	Ⓑ	Ⓒ	Ⓓ	30.	Ⓐ	Ⓑ	Ⓒ	Ⓓ
6.	Ⓐ	Ⓑ	Ⓒ	Ⓓ	31.	Ⓐ	Ⓑ	Ⓒ	Ⓓ
7.	Ⓐ	Ⓑ	Ⓒ	Ⓓ	32.	Ⓐ	Ⓑ	Ⓒ	Ⓓ
8.	Ⓐ	Ⓑ	Ⓒ	Ⓓ	33.	Ⓐ	Ⓑ	Ⓒ	Ⓓ
9.	Ⓐ	Ⓑ	Ⓒ	Ⓓ	34.	Ⓐ	Ⓑ	Ⓒ	Ⓓ
10.	Ⓐ	Ⓑ	Ⓒ	Ⓓ	35.	Ⓐ	Ⓑ	Ⓒ	Ⓓ
11.	Ⓐ	Ⓑ	Ⓒ	Ⓓ	36.	Ⓐ	Ⓑ	Ⓒ	Ⓓ
12.	Ⓐ	Ⓑ	Ⓒ	Ⓓ	37.	Ⓐ	Ⓑ	Ⓒ	Ⓓ
13.	Ⓐ	Ⓑ	Ⓒ	Ⓓ	38.	Ⓐ	Ⓑ	Ⓒ	Ⓓ
14.	Ⓐ	Ⓑ	Ⓒ	Ⓓ	39.	Ⓐ	Ⓑ	Ⓒ	Ⓓ
15.	Ⓐ	Ⓑ	Ⓒ	Ⓓ	40.	Ⓐ	Ⓑ	Ⓒ	Ⓓ
16.	Ⓐ	Ⓑ	Ⓒ	Ⓓ	41.	Ⓐ	Ⓑ	Ⓒ	Ⓓ
17.	Ⓐ	Ⓑ	Ⓒ	Ⓓ	42.	Ⓐ	Ⓑ	Ⓒ	Ⓓ
18.	Ⓐ	Ⓑ	Ⓒ	Ⓓ	43.	Ⓐ	Ⓑ	Ⓒ	Ⓓ
19.	Ⓐ	Ⓑ	Ⓒ	Ⓓ	44.	Ⓐ	Ⓑ	Ⓒ	Ⓓ
20.	Ⓐ	Ⓑ	Ⓒ	Ⓓ	45.	Ⓐ	Ⓑ	Ⓒ	Ⓓ
21.	Ⓐ	Ⓑ	Ⓒ	Ⓓ	46.	Ⓐ	Ⓑ	Ⓒ	Ⓓ
22.	Ⓐ	Ⓑ	Ⓒ	Ⓓ	47.	Ⓐ	Ⓑ	Ⓒ	Ⓓ
23.	Ⓐ	Ⓑ	Ⓒ	Ⓓ	48.	Ⓐ	Ⓑ	Ⓒ	Ⓓ
24.	Ⓐ	Ⓑ	Ⓒ	Ⓓ	49.	Ⓐ	Ⓑ	Ⓒ	Ⓓ
25.	Ⓐ	Ⓑ	Ⓒ	Ⓓ	50.	Ⓐ	Ⓑ	Ⓒ	Ⓓ

V&S Publisher, Head Office: F-2/16 Ansari Road, Daryaganj, New Delhi-110002, Ph: 011-23240026-27, Email:info@vspublishers.com
Regional Office: 5-1-707/1, Brij Bhawan (Beside Central Bank of India Lane) Bank Street, Koti, Hyderabad-500 095,
Ph: 040-24737290, Email: vspublishershyd@gmail.com

OMR ANSWER SHEET

1. NAME (IN ENGLISH CAPITAL LETTERS ONLY)

2. FATHER'S NAME (IN ENGLISH CAPITAL LETTERS ONLY)

Students must write and darken the respective circles completely for School Code, Class and Roll No. columns, othewise their Answer Sheets will not be evaluated.

3. SCHOOL CODE

(A) (A) (0) (0) (0) (0)
(B) (B) (1) (1) (1) (1)
(C) (C) (2) (2) (2) (2)
(D) (D) (3) (3) (3) (3)
(E) (E) (4) (4) (4) (4)
(F) (F) (5) (5) (5) (5)
(G) (G) (6) (6) (6) (6)
(H) (H) (7) (7) (7) (7)
(I) (I) (8) (8) (8) (8)
(J) (J) (9) (9) (9) (9)
(K) (K)
(L) (L)
(M) (M)
(N) (N)
(O) (O)
(P) (P)
(Q) (Q)
(R) (R)
(S) (S)
(T) (T)
(U) (U)
(V) (V)
(W) (W)
(X) (X)
(Y) (Y)
(Z) (Z)

4. % of Marks | Grade

In Last Class

Percentage	OR	Grade

(0) (0) (0)   (A)
(1) (1) (1)   (B)
(2) (2) (2)   (C)
(3) (3) (3)   (D)
(4) (4) (4)   (E)
(5) (5) (5)   (F)
(6) (6) (6)   (G)
(7) (7) (7)   (H)
(8) (8) (8)   (I)
(9) (9) (9)   (J)

5. CLASS

(0) (0)
(1) (1)
(2) (2)
   (4)
   (5)
   (6)
   (7)
   (8)
   (9)
   (M)
   (B)

6. ROLL NO.

(0) (0) (0)
(1) (1) (1)
(2) (2) (2)
(3) (3) (3)
(4) (4) (4)
(5) (5) (5)
(6) (6) (6)
(7) (7) (7)
(8) (8) (8)
(9) (9) (9)

7. GENDER

MALE ◯
FEMALE ◯

8. STREAM
(Only for Class XI and XII Students)

MATHEMATICS ◯
BIOLOGY ◯
OTHERS ◯

9. MARK YOUR ANSWERS WITH HB PENCIL/BALL POINT PEN (BLUE/BLACK)

1.	(A) (B) (C) (D)	26.	(A) (B) (C) (D)
2.	(A) (B) (C) (D)	27.	(A) (B) (C) (D)
3.	(A) (B) (C) (D)	28.	(A) (B) (C) (D)
4.	(A) (B) (C) (D)	29.	(A) (B) (C) (D)
5.	(A) (B) (C) (D)	30.	(A) (B) (C) (D)
6.	(A) (B) (C) (D)	31.	(A) (B) (C) (D)
7.	(A) (B) (C) (D)	32.	(A) (B) (C) (D)
8.	(A) (B) (C) (D)	33.	(A) (B) (C) (D)
9.	(A) (B) (C) (D)	34.	(A) (B) (C) (D)
10.	(A) (B) (C) (D)	35.	(A) (B) (C) (D)
11.	(A) (B) (C) (D)	36.	(A) (B) (C) (D)
12.	(A) (B) (C) (D)	37.	(A) (B) (C) (D)
13.	(A) (B) (C) (D)	38.	(A) (B) (C) (D)
14.	(A) (B) (C) (D)	39.	(A) (B) (C) (D)
15.	(A) (B) (C) (D)	40.	(A) (B) (C) (D)
16.	(A) (B) (C) (D)	41.	(A) (B) (C) (D)
17.	(A) (B) (C) (D)	42.	(A) (B) (C) (D)
18.	(A) (B) (C) (D)	43.	(A) (B) (C) (D)
19.	(A) (B) (C) (D)	44.	(A) (B) (C) (D)
20.	(A) (B) (C) (D)	45.	(A) (B) (C) (D)
21.	(A) (B) (C) (D)	46.	(A) (B) (C) (D)
22.	(A) (B) (C) (D)	47.	(A) (B) (C) (D)
23.	(A) (B) (C) (D)	48.	(A) (B) (C) (D)
24.	(A) (B) (C) (D)	49.	(A) (B) (C) (D)
25.	(A) (B) (C) (D)	50.	(A) (B) (C) (D)

V&S Publisher, Head Office: F-2/16 Ansari Road, Daryaganj, New Delhi-110002, Ph: 011-23240026-27, Email:info@vspublishers.com
Regional Office: 5-1-707/1, Brij Bhawan (Beside Central Bank of India Lane) Bank Street, Koti, Hyderabad-500 095,
Ph: 040-24737290, Email: vspublishershyd@gmail.com

OMR ANSWER SHEET

1. NAME (IN ENGLISH CAPITAL LETTERS ONLY)

2. FATHER'S NAME (IN ENGLISH CAPITAL LETTERS ONLY)

Students must write and darken the respective circles completely for School Code, Class and Roll No. columns, othewise their Answer Sheets will not be evaluated.

3. SCHOOL CODE

(A) (A) (0) (0) (0) (0)
(B) (B) (1) (1) (1) (1)
(C) (C) (2) (2) (2) (2)
(D) (D) (3) (3) (3) (3)
(E) (E) (4) (4) (4) (4)
(F) (F) (5) (5) (5) (5)
(G) (G) (6) (6) (6) (6)
(H) (H) (7) (7) (7) (7)
(I) (I) (8) (8) (8) (8)
(J) (J) (9) (9) (9) (9)
(K) (K)
(L) (L)
(M) (M)
(N) (N)
(O) (O)
(P) (P)
(Q) (Q)
(R) (R)
(S) (S)
(T) (T)
(U) (U)
(V) (V)
(W) (W)
(X) (X)
(Y) (Y)
(Z) (Z)

4. % of Marks | Grade

In Last Class

Percentage OR Grade

(0) (0) (0)   (A)
(1) (1) (1)   (B)
(2) (2) (2)   (C)
(3) (3) (3)   (D)
(4) (4) (4)   (E)
(5) (5) (5)   (F)
(6) (6) (6)   (G)
(7) (7) (7)   (H)
(8) (8) (8)   (I)
(9) (9) (9)   (J)

5. CLASS

(0) (0)
(1) (1)
(2) (2)
    (4)
    (5)
    (6)
    (7)
    (8)
    (9)
    (M)
    (B)

6. ROLL NO.

(0) (0) (0)
(1) (1) (1)
(2) (2) (2)
(3) (3) (3)
(4) (4) (4)
(5) (5) (5)
(6) (6) (6)
(7) (7) (7)
(8) (8) (8)
(9) (9) (9)

7. GENDER

MALE ○
FEMALE ○

8. STREAM
(Only for Class XI and XII Students)

MATHEMATICS ○
BIOLOGY ○
OTHERS ○

9. MARK YOUR ANSWERS WITH HB PENCIL/BALL POINT PEN (BLUE/BLACK)

No.	A	B	C	D	No.	A	B	C	D
1.	(A)	(B)	(C)	(D)	26.	(A)	(B)	(C)	(D)
2.	(A)	(B)	(C)	(D)	27.	(A)	(B)	(C)	(D)
3.	(A)	(B)	(C)	(D)	28.	(A)	(B)	(C)	(D)
4.	(A)	(B)	(C)	(D)	29.	(A)	(B)	(C)	(D)
5.	(A)	(B)	(C)	(D)	30.	(A)	(B)	(C)	(D)
6.	(A)	(B)	(C)	(D)	31.	(A)	(B)	(C)	(D)
7.	(A)	(B)	(C)	(D)	32.	(A)	(B)	(C)	(D)
8.	(A)	(B)	(C)	(D)	33.	(A)	(B)	(C)	(D)
9.	(A)	(B)	(C)	(D)	34.	(A)	(B)	(C)	(D)
10.	(A)	(B)	(C)	(D)	35.	(A)	(B)	(C)	(D)
11.	(A)	(B)	(C)	(D)	36.	(A)	(B)	(C)	(D)
12.	(A)	(B)	(C)	(D)	37.	(A)	(B)	(C)	(D)
13.	(A)	(B)	(C)	(D)	38.	(A)	(B)	(C)	(D)
14.	(A)	(B)	(C)	(D)	39.	(A)	(B)	(C)	(D)
15.	(A)	(B)	(C)	(D)	40.	(A)	(B)	(C)	(D)
16.	(A)	(B)	(C)	(D)	41.	(A)	(B)	(C)	(D)
17.	(A)	(B)	(C)	(D)	42.	(A)	(B)	(C)	(D)
18.	(A)	(B)	(C)	(D)	43.	(A)	(B)	(C)	(D)
19.	(A)	(B)	(C)	(D)	44.	(A)	(B)	(C)	(D)
20.	(A)	(B)	(C)	(D)	45.	(A)	(B)	(C)	(D)
21.	(A)	(B)	(C)	(D)	46.	(A)	(B)	(C)	(D)
22.	(A)	(B)	(C)	(D)	47.	(A)	(B)	(C)	(D)
23.	(A)	(B)	(C)	(D)	48.	(A)	(B)	(C)	(D)
24.	(A)	(B)	(C)	(D)	49.	(A)	(B)	(C)	(D)
25.	(A)	(B)	(C)	(D)	50.	(A)	(B)	(C)	(D)

V&S Publisher, Head Office: F-2/16 Ansari Road, Daryaganj, New Delhi-110002, Ph: 011-23240026-27, Email:info@vspublishers.com
Regional Office: 5-1-707/1, Brij Bhawan (Beside Central Bank of India Lane) Bank Street, Koti, Hyderabad-500 095,
Ph: 040-24737290, Email: vspublishershyd@gmail.com

OMR ANSWER SHEET

1. NAME (IN ENGLISH CAPITAL LETTERS ONLY)

2. FATHER'S NAME (IN ENGLISH CAPITAL LETTERS ONLY)

Students must write and darken the respective circles completely for School Code, Class and Roll No. columns, othewise their Answer Sheets will not be evaluated.

3. SCHOOL CODE

Columns: (A)–(Z), (A)–(Z), (0)–(9), (0)–(9), (0)–(9), (0)–(9)

4. % of Marks / Grade

In Last Class

Percentage OR Grade

Percentage columns: (0)–(9), (0)–(9), (0)–(9)
Grade: (A)(B)(C)(D)(E)(F)(G)(H)(I)(J)

5. CLASS

Columns: (0)(1)(2), (0)(1)(2)(4)(5)(6)(7)(8)(9)(M)(B)

6. ROLL NO.

Columns: (0)–(9), (0)–(9), (0)–(9)

7. GENDER

MALE ◯
FEMALE ◯

8. STREAM
(Only for Class XI and XII Students)

MATHEMATICS ◯
BIOLOGY ◯
OTHERS ◯

9. MARK YOUR ANSWERS WITH HB PENCIL/BALL POINT PEN (BLUE/BLACK)

No.	A	B	C	D	No.	A	B	C	D
1.	Ⓐ	Ⓑ	Ⓒ	Ⓓ	26.	Ⓐ	Ⓑ	Ⓒ	Ⓓ
2.	Ⓐ	Ⓑ	Ⓒ	Ⓓ	27.	Ⓐ	Ⓑ	Ⓒ	Ⓓ
3.	Ⓐ	Ⓑ	Ⓒ	Ⓓ	28.	Ⓐ	Ⓑ	Ⓒ	Ⓓ
4.	Ⓐ	Ⓑ	Ⓒ	Ⓓ	29.	Ⓐ	Ⓑ	Ⓒ	Ⓓ
5.	Ⓐ	Ⓑ	Ⓒ	Ⓓ	30.	Ⓐ	Ⓑ	Ⓒ	Ⓓ
6.	Ⓐ	Ⓑ	Ⓒ	Ⓓ	31.	Ⓐ	Ⓑ	Ⓒ	Ⓓ
7.	Ⓐ	Ⓑ	Ⓒ	Ⓓ	32.	Ⓐ	Ⓑ	Ⓒ	Ⓓ
8.	Ⓐ	Ⓑ	Ⓒ	Ⓓ	33.	Ⓐ	Ⓑ	Ⓒ	Ⓓ
9.	Ⓐ	Ⓑ	Ⓒ	Ⓓ	34.	Ⓐ	Ⓑ	Ⓒ	Ⓓ
10.	Ⓐ	Ⓑ	Ⓒ	Ⓓ	35.	Ⓐ	Ⓑ	Ⓒ	Ⓓ
11.	Ⓐ	Ⓑ	Ⓒ	Ⓓ	36.	Ⓐ	Ⓑ	Ⓒ	Ⓓ
12.	Ⓐ	Ⓑ	Ⓒ	Ⓓ	37.	Ⓐ	Ⓑ	Ⓒ	Ⓓ
13.	Ⓐ	Ⓑ	Ⓒ	Ⓓ	38.	Ⓐ	Ⓑ	Ⓒ	Ⓓ
14.	Ⓐ	Ⓑ	Ⓒ	Ⓓ	39.	Ⓐ	Ⓑ	Ⓒ	Ⓓ
15.	Ⓐ	Ⓑ	Ⓒ	Ⓓ	40.	Ⓐ	Ⓑ	Ⓒ	Ⓓ
16.	Ⓐ	Ⓑ	Ⓒ	Ⓓ	41.	Ⓐ	Ⓑ	Ⓒ	Ⓓ
17.	Ⓐ	Ⓑ	Ⓒ	Ⓓ	42.	Ⓐ	Ⓑ	Ⓒ	Ⓓ
18.	Ⓐ	Ⓑ	Ⓒ	Ⓓ	43.	Ⓐ	Ⓑ	Ⓒ	Ⓓ
19.	Ⓐ	Ⓑ	Ⓒ	Ⓓ	44.	Ⓐ	Ⓑ	Ⓒ	Ⓓ
20.	Ⓐ	Ⓑ	Ⓒ	Ⓓ	45.	Ⓐ	Ⓑ	Ⓒ	Ⓓ
21.	Ⓐ	Ⓑ	Ⓒ	Ⓓ	46.	Ⓐ	Ⓑ	Ⓒ	Ⓓ
22.	Ⓐ	Ⓑ	Ⓒ	Ⓓ	47.	Ⓐ	Ⓑ	Ⓒ	Ⓓ
23.	Ⓐ	Ⓑ	Ⓒ	Ⓓ	48.	Ⓐ	Ⓑ	Ⓒ	Ⓓ
24.	Ⓐ	Ⓑ	Ⓒ	Ⓓ	49.	Ⓐ	Ⓑ	Ⓒ	Ⓓ
25.	Ⓐ	Ⓑ	Ⓒ	Ⓓ	50.	Ⓐ	Ⓑ	Ⓒ	Ⓓ

V&S Publisher, Head Office: F-2/16 Ansari Road, Daryaganj, New Delhi-110002, Ph: 011-23240026-27, Email:info@vspublishers.com
Regional Office: 5-1-707/1, Brij Bhawan (Beside Central Bank of India Lane) Bank Street, Koti, Hyderabad-500 095,
Ph: 040-24737290, Email: vspublishershyd@gmail.com

OMR ANSWER SHEET

1. NAME (IN ENGLISH CAPITAL LETTERS ONLY)

2. FATHER'S NAME (IN ENGLISH CAPITAL LETTERS ONLY)

Students must write and darken the respective circles completely for School Code, Class and Roll No. columns, otehwise their Answer Sheets will not be evaluated.

3. SCHOOL CODE

(A) (B) (C) (D) (E) (F) (G) (H) (I) (J) (K) (L) (M) (N) (O) (P) (Q) (R) (S) (T) (U) (V) (W) (X) (Y) (Z)

(A) (B) (C) (D) (E) (F) (G) (H) (I) (J) (K) (L) (M) (N) (O) (P) (Q) (R) (S) (T) (U) (V) (W) (X) (Y) (Z)

(0) (1) (2) (3) (4) (5) (6) (7) (8) (9)

(0) (1) (2) (3) (4) (5) (6) (7) (8) (9)

(0) (1) (2) (3) (4) (5) (6) (7) (8) (9)

(0) (1) (2) (3) (4) (5) (6) (7) (8) (9)

4. % of Marks | Grade
In Last Class

Percentage	OR	Grade

(0) (1) (2) (3) (4) (5) (6) (7) (8) (9)
(0) (1) (2) (3) (4) (5) (6) (7) (8) (9)
(0) (1) (2) (3) (4) (5) (6) (7) (8) (9)

(A) (B) (C) (D) (E) (F) (G) (H) (I) (J)

5. CLASS

(0) (1) (2)

(0) (1) (2) (4) (5) (6) (7) (8) (9) (M) (B)

6. ROLL NO.

(0) (1) (2) (3) (4) (5) (6) (7) (8) (9)

(0) (1) (2) (3) (4) (5) (6) (7) (8) (9)

(0) (1) (2) (3) (4) (5) (6) (7) (8) (9)

7. GENDER

| MALE | ○ |
| FEMALE | ○ |

8. STREAM
(Only for Class XI and XII Students)

MATHEMATICS	○
BIOLOGY	○
OTHERS	○

9. MARK YOUR ANSWERS WITH HB PENCIL/BALL POINT PEN (BLUE/BLACK)

1. (A) (B) (C) (D)   26. (A) (B) (C) (D)
2. (A) (B) (C) (D)   27. (A) (B) (C) (D)
3. (A) (B) (C) (D)   28. (A) (B) (C) (D)
4. (A) (B) (C) (D)   29. (A) (B) (C) (D)
5. (A) (B) (C) (D)   30. (A) (B) (C) (D)
6. (A) (B) (C) (D)   31. (A) (B) (C) (D)
7. (A) (B) (C) (D)   32. (A) (B) (C) (D)
8. (A) (B) (C) (D)   33. (A) (B) (C) (D)
9. (A) (B) (C) (D)   34. (A) (B) (C) (D)
10. (A) (B) (C) (D)   35. (A) (B) (C) (D)
11. (A) (B) (C) (D)   36. (A) (B) (C) (D)
12. (A) (B) (C) (D)   37. (A) (B) (C) (D)
13. (A) (B) (C) (D)   38. (A) (B) (C) (D)
14. (A) (B) (C) (D)   39. (A) (B) (C) (D)
15. (A) (B) (C) (D)   40. (A) (B) (C) (D)
16. (A) (B) (C) (D)   41. (A) (B) (C) (D)
17. (A) (B) (C) (D)   42. (A) (B) (C) (D)
18. (A) (B) (C) (D)   43. (A) (B) (C) (D)
19. (A) (B) (C) (D)   44. (A) (B) (C) (D)
20. (A) (B) (C) (D)   45. (A) (B) (C) (D)
21. (A) (B) (C) (D)   46. (A) (B) (C) (D)
22. (A) (B) (C) (D)   47. (A) (B) (C) (D)
23. (A) (B) (C) (D)   48. (A) (B) (C) (D)
24. (A) (B) (C) (D)   49. (A) (B) (C) (D)
25. (A) (B) (C) (D)   50. (A) (B) (C) (D)

V&S Publisher, Head Office: F-2/16 Ansari Road, Daryaganj, New Delhi-110002, Ph: 011-23240026-27, Email:info@vspublishers.com
Regional Office: 5-1-707/1, Brij Bhawan (Beside Central Bank of India Lane) Bank Street, Koti, Hyderabad-500 095,
Ph: 040-24737290, Email: vspublishershyd@gmail.com